D0190945

TRUST
AND TEAMS

Putting Servant Leadership to Work

JANE L. FRYAR

SAINT LOUIS

1 2 3 4 5 6 7 8 9 10   11 10 09 08 07 06 05 04 03 02

Contents

Preface

This book takes the Holy Bible as God's Word and seeks to draw from it lessons on leadership. At the same time, I will apply here what we might call "First Article knowledge" to leadership processes in the church. This kind of knowledge comes from researchers who study the world God created. While it is not theology drawn directly from the Bible, it is truth that can support and augment theology. Over the past six decades or so, scholars in organizational studies have developed many ideas helpful to those who lead God's people. Built on sound principles of psychology and sociology, leadership theory can guide those who want to lead others skillfully and courageously.

Some in the Christian community have rejected all organizational theories because a few scholars' ideas clash with the truths revealed in the Holy Scriptures. When theories contradict Holy Scripture, we must reject them. They are dangerous to faith and life in the body of Christ. Yet while filtering out the "camels" and even the "gnats" that Jesus warned us about (Matthew 23:24), Christian leaders will want to take advantage of ideas and methods that can strengthen their leadership skills and abilities. Our Lord wants to equip us in every way "with everything good for doing His will," even as He works in us "what is pleasing to Him" (Hebrews 13:21). He does this, in part, through "First Article" truths.

This book expands on the concepts presented in my previous book, *Servant Leadership: Setting Leaders Free* (CPH, 2001). Here I explore the implications of servant leadership for developing trust and teams in the context of church work. Though I see these things as congruent with Scripture and worthy of study, other models also grace the pages of the Holy Scriptures. I pray that this brief study will encourage others to explore what Scripture has to say about leadership in the church. I also pray that it will provoke Christian leaders to dig into more of the organizational scholarship that is available to us.

God wants His people to be not only well-fed but well-led. Every leader in the church I have ever known has wanted to lead God's people well. May God grant us wisdom to discern the truth about leadership—wherever we may find it. And may He grant us grace to apply that truth for the good of the church and the glory of our Savior!

1

As We Begin

A whole book—on trust? On trust in the church? Why?

It's a fair question, one with some challenging answers. Consider these pieces of the puzzle.

First, as Robert D. Putnam contends in his influential study *Bowling Alone: The Collapse and Revival of American Community,* society as a whole has grown less inclined to join in on the kinds of volunteer efforts that, in the past, have made life more civil and contributed to our individual and common well-being. The generation of joiners who created Kiwanis, the United Way, Rotary, the Lions Club, the Girl Scouts, and other civic organizations is retreating into history. Who will replace them? *Only in high-trust environments can leaders recruit the eager support they need to achieve worthy goals.*

What does this mean in the church? Perhaps the decline in volunteerism has dented the dreams you've had for your congregation too. Can we trace all this decline back to distrust? Of course not. Still, trust is a firm prerequisite. We in the church need to develop the high-trust environments that make it possible to recruit motivated and skilled volunteers—not to mention gifted and compassionate pastors and other professional workers.

Second, we have all heard for several decades now that confidence in society's stabilizing institutions has eroded. Government. Business. Public education. The media. All have watched their credibility seep away. Meanwhile, the growing complexity of our problems makes it evident that no individual working alone can reasonably hope to offer a viable cure. Only as we collaborate can we begin to address our culture's difficulties. *Trust provides the foundation of support that highly motivated, collaborative teams need for top performance.*

What does this mean in the church? We have not escaped the crisis of confidence that has hobbled other once-respected institutions. We have lived through our own scandals, suffered from our own ineptitude. Our members and their families face their own set of complexities. We, too, need the kind of foundational trust that makes collaboration possible! Once we recruit workers, an atmosphere of trust will encourage their participation and help make their contributions the best they can be.

Third, no one can doubt that the pace of change has quickened in recent decades. What works well today will likely wind up in next week's garage sale. Leaders have never been able to amass all the facts they might want to have as they make decisions. Complexity and change force leaders into decisions with consequences they can't control. *Excessive and ongoing distrust severely limits leaders' options—at the very time when rapid change makes the generation of multiple options necessary.*

What does this mean in the church? Some things— the most important things—don't change: Christ's death and resurrection for our sins. Our Father's constant care and protection. The Holy Spirit's continual faith-building work in our hearts through His Word, in our Baptism, and at the Holy Supper. These and other truths of the Christian faith remain immutable.

However, the challenges facing our leaders—especially our pastors—as they minister to hurting people continue to grow. Not every ministry decision has one best answer. Not every pastor has the luxury of meditating for a week over even momentous problems and choices. Chronic and excessive distrust easily makes difficult decisions even harder by limiting options. Distrust provokes the kind of second-guessing that stimulates grousing and gossip. This creates more distrust, and on it goes.

We need the kind of trust that opens options while providing the safety of mutual accountability needed both by leaders and by members in the church today. And God, working through His Word and Sacraments, gives grace to create the atmosphere of trust we need.

In summary, trust has a lot to do with recruiting volunteers and professional workers in the church. It helps determine how hard volunteers work. It influences the results volunteers' efforts produce. Trust opens the options needed if we want to solve complex problems. Finally, trust makes relationships more comfortable. Would you rather spend time with colleagues who trust and respect you or with inquisitors who suspect your every motive and question your decisions? Research shows that people won't stay long in organizations where mistrust pollutes the atmosphere. Shouldn't the church be a safe place? A place of unity and love? Wouldn't Jesus want that (John 13:35; 17:20–23)?

Trust and Servant Leadership

As I have studied trust and the ways it gets created and flourishes in organizations, I have become convinced that these issues dovetail neatly with the ideals of servant leadership. The intersection excites me and encourages me. I hope you find it exciting and encouraging as well.

My previous book, *Servant Leadership: Setting Leaders Free*, outlines the ideals of servant leadership and their implications for the church. There I laid out the theological issues and built the framework for an overall understanding of servant leadership in the context of the congregation and other Christian organizations.

Let's briefly review five of the central values of servant leadership.[1] As we do that, keep in mind the dismay expressed by Don Frick, an expert on servant-leadership issues, as he notes the many requests he receives for a quick explanation of servant leadership. Such an explanation "may not be possible," he observes, "because [servant leadership] describes a process of inner growth and outer consequences that, though based on some universal principles, must necessarily take unique expression within particular individuals and institutions. . . . [When] servant leadership is reduced to a collection of admirable qualities and learned skills that are displayed in organizational settings, it is all too easy to forget that servant leadership is, first, about deep identity" (p. 354).

Not a gimmick. Not a quick fix like the power suit, power lunch, or power nap. Servant leadership grows out of a leader's core identity. Servant leaders align their actions with their attitudes and values—attitudes and values that lie at the core of their being.

We are attempting to describe the "unique expression" servant leadership takes or could take "within particular individuals and institutions," as Frick suggests—in this case, individual leaders, congregations, and other organizations in the Christian church. Though I believe leaders in any Christian congregation or organization could find much food for thought here, the examples I have chosen grow out of my personal experiences and the experiences of several of my brothers and sisters in the Lutheran faith who graciously read the manuscript that became this book and shared stories and insights of their own to illustrate.[2] My church body, The Lutheran

Church—Missouri Synod, is a Christ-centered, Bible-based church body, steeped in conservative doctrine. We celebrate a rich sacramental and liturgical heritage. We also struggle with issues of trust—individually, in our congregations, and as a church body. We are justified by Christ, but not yet fully sanctified!

Despite our corporate sins and failures, we know something about the idea that doing grows out of being, out of identity. We believe that in Baptism God has graciously united us to the death and resurrection of His Son. We now live in Christ (Romans 6; Ephesians 1), and this new identity makes it possible for us to serve one another in love (Galatians 5:13). Our new identity also animates those who lead in the church. It creates the servant hearts the Lord wants in His representatives.

Servant leaders in the church can avoid quick fixes, gimmicks, and management fads. We can rely instead on foundational, bedrock truths as we lead, realizing that the Holy Spirit has taught them to us and makes it possible for us to live them out in our relationships. Here, then, are the five values I have identified and applied to servant leadership in the church:

- Servant leaders serve. In fact, they place a premium on service. Partly this involves helping followers attain their own personal goals. In addition, servant leaders want to serve in such a way that their organizations thrive for the good of all organizational stakeholders.

- Servant leaders lead. They believe the Creator intended all individuals to live lives of significance and meaning. Thus, servant leaders use their God-given experience, intuition, foresight, insight, and wisdom to cast a compelling, encouraging, and motivating vision of the future that energizes followers.

- Servant leaders value the freedom and dignity of the individual. Therefore, servant leaders rely primarily on the art of persuasion to create consensus and a sense of community in Christian congregations, instead of trying to force compliance by coercion or manipulation.

- Servant leaders believe God has gifted each of His people with unique and precious talents and abilities. Thus, servant leaders seek to develop followers' gifts, appreciating their strengths and empowering them to use their gifts to their maximum potential.

- Servant leaders value wholeness and growth and want these for their followers and themselves. Thus, they value confession and absolution as a treasure Christ has given to the church. They esteem healing and learning as beneficial and necessary gifts of God in Christ. They model these in their own lives, and they find ways to engage their organizations and followers in the processes of healing and growth as well.

Note that these are not a collection of random values; each strand is interwoven with the others to form a tapestry. The values thus created in a servant leader's life show themselves in attitudes that lead to specific actions. Robert Russell, in his work for the Regent University Center for Leadership Studies, has provided a working definition of servant leadership that illustrates the interlocking nature of these values, attitudes, and actions:

> Servant leaders *seek not to be served, but rather to serve*. They view leadership positions as opportunities to help, support, and aid other people. Servant leaders create *trusting* work environments in which *people are highly appreciated*. They *listen* to and *encourage* followers. Servant leaders *visibly model* appropriate behavior and function as effective *teachers*. They have a high degree of *credibility* because of their *honesty, integrity*, and *competence*. These persons have a clear leadership *vision* and implement *pioneering* approaches to work. Servant leaders are also conscientious *stewards* of resources. They have good *communications* with followers and exercise ethical *persuasion* as a means of *influence*. Servant leaders invite others to participate in carrying out their leadership vision. They *empower* people by enabling them to perform at their best and by *delegating* decision-making responsibilities. Overall, servant leaders provide direction and guidance by assuming the role of attendant to humanity. (Emphases original)

In the chapters that follow, we will explore each of these values as they intersect with issues of trust in Christian churches and institutions. I pray that the Lord will use the truths He has given us through the minds and work of organizational scholars, combining it with the revealed truth of His Word and the conviction of His Holy Spirit, more fully to equip all who—by His grace—lead others in the church in any way. May He work true Christlikeness in us, more and more, so that our leadership will bring honor to Him and peace and comfort to the souls for whom He died!

 Focus on Trust

1. How would you characterize the level of trust in your congregation or organization? How has it changed over the years? How do you know?

2. In what ways does servant leadership differ from the flavor-of-the-month management gimmicks that seem to come and go in the popular press?

3. How would you define servant leadership for someone who had never come across the term before?

4. Reread the five servant leader values on pages 12–13. Which of these do you find encouraging? Why? Do you disagree with or wonder about any of them? Explain.

5. In what ways do you currently live as a servant

leader? In what aspects of servant leadership would you like to grow?

2

Are You Being Served?

When department store clerks in London ask customers this question, they mean much the same thing as clerks in the United States who ask, "Have you been waited on?" What a great question, though, for leaders from any country to ask constituents: "Are you being served?" How do you think your constituents would answer if you were to ask them that question? Think about your own leadership and about the members of your organization as you reread the first value of servant leadership:

> Servant leaders serve. In fact, they place a premium on service. Partly, this involves helping followers attain their personal goals. In addition, servant leaders want to serve in such a way that their organizations thrive for the good of all organizational stakeholders.

The True Test of Servant Leadership

Robert K. Greenleaf, the business executive and thinker who has popularized the idea of servant leadership, proposes a test for servant leadership not unlike the question "Are you being served?" Greenleaf believes that the difference between servant leaders and others hinges on the idea of service:

> The difference manifests itself in the care taken by the servant first to make sure that other people's highest priority needs are being served. The best test, and the most difficult to administer is this: Do those served grow as persons? Do they, while being served, become healthier, wiser, freer, more autonomous, more likely themselves to become servants? And what is the effect on the least privileged in society; will they benefit, or, at least, not be further deprived? (*Servant Leadership,* p. 13)

Can you see from these questions that servant leadership is not at its heart a title, a uniform, or a job description? Ken Melrose, the highly respected CEO of Toro, Incorporated, goes so far as to assert that leadership is not a position at all. He believes, instead, that leadership is a combination of something we *are* (he calls this "character") and some things we *do* (he calls this "competence"). Melrose believes that if we think of leadership in terms of position, it's "almost impossible to develop an atmosphere of trust" ("Leader as Servant," p. 10).[3]

Perhaps this is true because the minute an office holder begins to focus on his position and to demand the honor and respect rightly due him because of it, thoughts of service and of followers' needs get lost because of the change in focus from others to self. Leadership is a trust-based relationship. It's a service that leaders offer but cannot force upon followers. It's an honor followers give to the leaders chosen because the followers believe in the leaders' capacity to serve the followers' needs.

A friend tells the story of the misery her family lived through during her childhood and adolescence. Her dad was an alcoholic, verbally abusive, and sometimes physically abusive when he was drinking. Everyone in her church knew about the problem—it was hard not to know given several public episodes. But no one offered help. The wall of silence that often imprisons those in alcoholic family systems stood firm.

One day, after my friend had gone away to the university, she met a classmate whose father served as pastor at a church near my friend's hometown. Over Christmas break the two drove home together, and my friend ended up pouring out her heart to the pastor, asking him for help. He prayed with her and offered to meet with the family on one condition—that someone get permission from the family's own pastor first.

The first task, as my friend saw it, lay in getting her family to admit they needed help. While she worked on that, the hometown pastor somehow found out about her plan. He appeared on the family's front steps the next night, unannounced. My friend describes the resulting confrontation this way:

It was barely civil. He barged in, obviously angry and determined to have his say. He practically shouted the whole time. "You're my members! If you have a problem, you come to me!" Mom cried. She was so ashamed. Dad left—to go to the tavern. We didn't leave the church after that. It was a small town and there was no place else to go. But we stopped attending as often. It was eight years before my family finally got help. Eight years! By that time Pastor ____ had moved. I had known before that night he didn't have the skills to help us. But he proved it to the whole family, that's for sure!

If you have to demand the right to serve or to lead, you've already lost the trust you need to do so.

What Is Trust? Where Does It Come From?

What do we mean by the word *trust*? Just what is it anyhow? And how does a leader know when she has it and when she doesn't? Perhaps surprisingly, researchers who study trust in organizations have not agreed on one commonly accepted definition. Robert B. Shaw, in his book *Trust in the Balance: Building Successful Organizations on Results, Integrity, and Concern*, comes at the concept simply, proposing that trust is "the belief that those on whom we depend will meet our expectations" (p. 21). Trust assumes that others will not deliberately hurt us or take advantage of our reliance on them.

Other researchers affirm Shaw's definition, but offer several additional dimensions:

"Trust is the willingness of a party to be vulnerable to the actions of another party based on the expectation that the other will perform a particular action important to the trustor, [whether or not the trustor can] monitor or control that other party" (p. 559).

In their article "The Structure of Optimal Trust: Moral and Strategic Implications," business professors Andrew Wicks, Shawn Berman, and Thomas Jones suggest that trust therefore also involves "taking not-so-calculated risks. . . . Part of what it is to trust is not to have too many thoughts of possible betrayals" (p. 99). Furthermore, they see trust not as a static, permanent state of mind, but as a dynamic and continuous variable. Trust is not an either/or phenomenon. In fact, "one can both trust and distrust people at the same time" (p. 101).

Pulling this all together, we can say that trust involves three separate, interacting dimensions:

- A highly calculative and cognitive dimension that asks, "How do I know the other person will come through for me?"

- An emotional bond that makes it possible for people to move beyond rational prediction. This dimension enables a "leap of faith" that one's trust will be met with honor and acknowledges that the leader may sometimes know better than the followers.

- A belief in the moral character and the goodwill of the trustee.

Trustworthiness, then, has three corresponding dimensions:

- Competence—the ability of the trustee to live up to the trustor's confidence.

- Willingness—the trustee's desire to live up to the trustor's confidence.

- Character—the moral commitment by the trustee to live up to the trustor's confidence regardless of the difficulties that it may involve or the price that may have to be paid.

As we have seen, trust involves elements of risk-taking, vulnerability, calculation, emotion, honor, character, and confidence. Trust is also contextual; it is shaped by the dynamics involved in particular social settings. We might see a leader as competent and meriting trust in some areas but not in others. This implies that the decision to trust doesn't always arise from personal knowledge of another's trustworthiness. For example, Morton Deutsch, in his seminal work *The Resolution of Conflict: Constructive and Destructive Processes,* has pointed out four other sources from which trust may grow:

- Confidence in existing social institutions that discourage untrustworthy behavior. (E.g., We trust a pastor just out of the seminary to shepherd us faithfully. Our trust comes, to a certain extent, from our trust in our church's seminaries and in the judicatory officials who guide new pastors.)

- Confidence in a third party who vouches for the other person. (E.g., We trust a new teacher in our parish school because we trust the principal who worked with her in a previous setting.)

- Confidence based on precedent. (E.g., If we've had a good experience with a previous pastor, we will likely trust our new one.)

- Confidence in the general trustworthiness of people we see as similar to ourselves. (E.g., I trust the new chairperson of my congregation's finance board because he works out at the same gym as I do and because he has belonged to my congregation for 10 years, though I've never had a conversation about spiritual matters with him.)

Most of the time in situations like these, we will give others the benefit of the doubt, investing trust in them initially for any or all of these reasons. However, complete trust comes (or fails to come) only after we have had the chance to get to know more about a person. Leaders lay the foundation of credibility brick by brick. There's no substitute for "promises made, promises kept" when it comes to the kind of deep trust leaders need as they enlist followers in a meaningful cause.

Do People Trust Me?

Good question. Perhaps it's human nature, but we tend to assume that since we consider ourselves trustworthy, others will see us as trustworthy too. But if we base our decisions and our actions on too many assumptions, we may face an abrupt and rude awakening.

As I noted earlier, leaders can't demand trust. Daniel Webster put it this way: "Confidence [in others] is not a thing to be produced by compulsion. Men cannot be forced into trust." Rather, leaders must inspire it.

How does that happen? Another good question. After several years of thought and in-depth research in organizations, James Kouzes and Barry Posner answer this way:

> Ultimately, all you can do is demonstrate your trust in others and have faith they will respond in kind. But take some initiative: don't wait for others to make the first move. The opening gambit always involves risk—and leaders find that risk well worth taking. (*The Leadership Challenge*, p. 178)

Their advice grows out of research showing that when leaders demonstrate trust in someone, it encourages that person to trust in return. Furthermore, people who believe they are trusted tend to act in trustworthy ways. But the converse also proves true: distrust breeds distrust.

The Lone Ranger vs. Michelangelo

Some leadership situations in the church call for one-on-one counseling. Many others, though, involve bringing the abilities and gifts of many members together to accomplish a mutual goal. Western culture perpetuates the myth of the heroic individual who rides onto the scene to accomplish great feats single-handedly. Actually, though, this hardly ever happens. People join hands and link arms to accomplish more than any individual could accomplish alone. Michelangelo worked with a team of 16 artists to paint the ceiling of the Sistine Chapel! Still, as organizational theorist Warren Bennis observes, "We tend to think of achievement in terms of the Great Man or the Great Woman, instead of the Great Group" ("The Secrets of Great Groups," online article).

If trust matters in dyadic (one-on-one) leader/follower relationships, it's crucial in leader/group relationships. The level of shared trust is key.

The Building Blocks of Trust

Leaders go first. Leaders venture out. Leaders assume the risks of trusting first. This begins with respect, but the respect must be genuine. If we rely on mere form, on gimmicks, on actions rather than on substance—on deeply held core beliefs and values—followers will soon sense it.

Can you see why servant leadership can prove so very difficult? Like all inside-out propositions, it must begin with a change of heart. Such a thorough change comes, I believe, from only one source—the Lord Jesus Himself. Lutheran theologians at the time of the Reformation wrote about "the righteousness of reason" or "civil righteousness." By this they meant those actions and thoughts that reasoning creatures of God, though fallen, could discern as morally right and could choose to perform, even apart from the indwelling Holy Spirit. Though non-Christians can—and have—seen the wisdom of servant leadership and adopted it in their organizational and personal lives, how many more possibilities for truly Christlike servant leadership open up when Christ Himself lives in us, motivating and empowering us! With St. Paul, Christians can exclaim, "I no longer live, but Christ lives in me!" (Galatians 2:20).

Even then, servant leadership is never easy. There is no ready recipe for developing trusting relationships. Beginning from a foundation of authentic, heartfelt respect, a servant leader moves outward toward building habits of trustworthy behaviors. Bennis has this to say:

> You have to be absolutely straight with people, never clever or cute, and you can't think you can

manipulate them. That doesn't mean you have to think they're all stars or that you have to agree with everything they do, but the relationship . . . ought to be for real. (*On Becoming a Leader*, p. 163)

In their article "Building and Maintaining Trust: The Role of Leadership," James Orlikoff and Mary Totten suggest seven leader characteristics that build trust. As you think about them, remember that servant-leadership behaviors grow outward from the leader's core identity. Notice how in each case being leads to doing (and not the other way around).

1. Commitment—show by your behaviors that you care about things beyond yourself.

2. Familiarity—build on multiple conversations and contacts with people so they begin to understand who you are and can predict how you will treat them.

3. Personal responsibility—acknowledge and take responsibility for your own behavior, admit your faults, confess your sins to those whom you hurt, and be willingly accountable instead of denying or blame-shifting.

4. Integrity—live out your values, your core identity, even when it's not comfortable or convenient; tell the truth, even when it hurts; do what you say you will do; keep your commitments.

5. Consistency—let people see the connection between your core identity, your words, and your actions; consistency breeds predictability and familiarity, which in turn breed trust.

6. Communication—open, honest communication is a cornerstone of building and maintaining trust; don't hide facts for the sake of expediency; when confidentiality keeps you from sharing, say so; keep people's confidences; remain willing to discuss even sensitive issues.

7. Forgiveness and reconciliation—this is a two-way process related to personal responsibility; when we abuse people's trust, we need to acknowledge what has happened, willingly deal with the consequences, and behave in ways that engender trust; we also need to be willing to discuss what's needed to rebuild trust and to move past the breach created by our own untrustworthy actions or those actions by which others have broken our trust in them.

As you can see, servant leadership requires changes in attitudes much more than it calls for structural changes in the ways groups organize themselves. To live as servant leaders, we must shed our egos again and again—as often as necessary—and fully embrace Ken Melrose's belief that "people perform best in an atmosphere of freedom and trust" ("Leader as Servant," p. 20). Or as organizational theorist Margaret Wheatley reminds us, "Honoring and trusting people has unleashed startlingly high levels of productivity and creativity" ("Goodbye, Command and Control," online article).

Where We've Been and Where We're Headed

Servant leadership begins with service. Serving others comes first, then leading. Soon enough in our servant leadership journey we see the critical importance of trust. James Kouzes writes:

> Credibility is the foundation of leadership. It's been reinforced so often that we've come to refer to it as "The First Law of Leadership." People won't believe the message if they don't believe in the messenger. People don't follow your technique. They follow you—your message and your embodiment of that message. ("Trust: The Invaluable Asset," p. 323)

As Max DePree has said in his article "The Leader's Legacy," leaders owe their followers respect and an understanding that "I cannot do very much without you." He goes on to say that leaders also owe followers the courtesy of pointing in the direction in which the group's goals and potential lie:

> As a leader, you've got to understand and explain the environment in which your organization and

your people are operating. You provide an agenda
of things to be working on that are going to have
an effect on your [joint] future. (online article)

Servant leaders serve. And servant leaders lead. The
kind of direction-setting DePree describes builds follower confidence, member trust. The next chapter will
explore issues of vision, trust, and servant leadership.

◎ Focus on Trust

1. Why does service come first in a discussion of servant leadership? How would you answer someone
   who asserts that leadership must come first?

2. In what sense is leadership . . .

   a. service leaders offer followers?

   b. an honor followers give their leader?

3. Skim back over the section "What Is Trust? Where
   Does It Come From?" Give examples from your
   own life in organizations to illustrate the various
   facets of trust introduced in this section.

4. Suppose you found yourself appointed leader of a
   group that had lost trust in its previous leader.
   What steps would you take immediately and over
   time to rebuild trust? How does any of this apply to
   groups you currently lead?

3

Seeing Is Believing

It changed my life. A few weeks after I moved to the St. Louis area, I found a new church home. Soon after, the leader of the congregation's evangelism team targeted me. He asked persistently that I sign on with the group that visited newcomers to the community. I had never done anything like that before. Honestly, the thought of ringing doorbells made my palms sweat. (For the first six months, I caught myself hoping that no one would come to the door!)

But on most nights that we went out we found at least one family at home and willing to listen. Afterward, we would return to the team leader's office for debriefing. We shared our stories of the evening's events. We planned the next week's strategies. We prayed together.

I lost a lot that year. I lost my fear of praying out loud. Somewhere along the line, I lost my fear that people would invite us inside their homes. I lost sleep over how to talk about Jesus with "religious" people who saw no real need for a personal Savior. And I lost control of my tear ducts every single time someone came to faith in that Savior.

Some nights the evangelism group prayed until one in the morning. Some weeks we went out on calls two evenings instead of just one. Sometimes we went to the doughnut stop or the pizza shop after we returned from our calls. Every week we grew stronger in our love for one another and for the Lord Jesus. It changed my life.

Trust and Well-Led Teams

Have you ever linked arms and hearts with a group set on a common goal, a joint purpose?

- A team competing in your state's high school basketball tournament?

- A crew determined to detassle 500 acres of corn in one day?

- A group committed to sharing Jesus with neighborhood kids through this year's VBS program?

- A family scraping to put every member through college?

- A crew erecting a high-rise office building in the heart of the city?

Whatever your project, can you recall the feelings that flooded over you as you reached your goal? How would you describe them? Exhilaration? Joy? Accomplishment? Pride? Thankfulness? As we hug each other or collect high fives from everyone on the team, we undoubtedly experience a sense of satisfaction. Joint effort toward a worthy goal makes us feel alive, connected, energized, confident. We're also usually ready to take on fresh challenges—given a few moments or days to rest first, that is.

The teams that Warren Bennis calls "Great Groups" energize their members in just these ways. Great Groups and the leaders of Great Groups (regardless of their personal style) generate and sustain trust. Their trust in one another and in their leadership allows members to accept dissent and to ride out the turbulence that naturally comes with the group process. This kind of trust grows, in part, as leaders provide direction and meaning. The leaders of Great Groups keep on reminding people of what's important and why their work makes a difference.

The leader of my evangelism team did this again and again, as he led our Bible studies, as he assigned tasks, as he chatted in the hallway after worship, and as he worked on my taxes—he was an accountant in "real life." However, regardless of which hat he wore at any given moment, he lived out of a single-minded purpose—to share Jesus. His actions grew from his heart's deepest values. *Being* came before *doing*. Remember, that's how servant leaders operate.

Besides knowing where they are going, leaders of Great Groups know where they want to take the group. According to James Kouzes and Barry Posner, leaders communicate this direction to their constituents:

If leaders are to be admired and respected, they must have the ability to see across the horizon of time and imagine what might be. We are not inclined to follow the directionless. Honest or not, leaders who don't know where they are going are likely to be joined by the rest of us for only as far as we ourselves can see. *(The Leadership Challenge,* p. 16)

Beyond Survival

A 1998 poll of congregations representing 29 denominations asked leaders about their goals for their congregation. Fifty-eight percent named "trying to keep the church going" as one of their top three priorities.[4] In a word, survival. Many, many churches are hurting. They feel the gravel giving way beneath their feet as they slip farther down the slope to oblivion. Not only churches feel this way. Respected business leader and consultant Charles Handy has this to say:

I ask a lot of leaders of organizations what it's all about. They usually say survival. I say that's only the first stage. If you're no use to anyone, you can't survive. What is it that you uniquely as an organization can contribute to the world? Most don't know the answer. Why then would you want to devote your life to an organization that can't give something special to the world? ("The Search for Meaning," online article)

Why indeed? My evangelism team knew we had something special to give the world—or to our part of it in south St. Louis, Missouri. What does your worship team, your Sunday school staff, your stewardship board have that it can uniquely contribute? How can we as leaders help our groups, our teams, to discover these unique, God-given, and life-enriching purposes?

Leaders play an important part in this visioning process. When we step out of the crowd to say *follow me,* our words imply that we know where we are headed, we see what the Spirit would have us do in Jesus' name and for His kingdom, and by grace we are committed to pouring our best efforts into achieving it. A vision, particularly a vision for mission in Christ's church, should, according to nonprofit-organization expert Terrie Temkin, involve "thinking big and thinking new" (p. 38).

A New Thing? In the Church!?

The very word *new* will frighten some followers. Even so, our Lord has been doing new things in new ways throughout history. Before Pentecost, for example, Jonah had been the only foreign missionary ever—or, at least, the only one the Old Testament tells us about. Yet look what the Holy Spirit did through Paul, Barnabas, Apollos, and the dozens, hundreds, and thousands who followed them in the years immediately after Pentecost! The Lord seems to have begun a new strategy altogether.

Especially when you expect reluctance ahead of time, it's important to carefully plan ways to bring the followers with misgivings along. In this regard, you may want to study the trust-building approach the early church took in Acts 11:19–26, 12:25–13:5, and 14:21–28. These texts from Acts reveal, among other things, the importance of accountability in building trust.

Trust and mutual accountability require that we reassure one another, especially those we lead, that a new vision, a change in approach or focus, does not mean a change in doctrine (Galatians 2:1–10). We treasure the unchanging truths of the faith. They form the foundation on which we stand! The pure Gospel is the dynamite of God (Romans 1:16) that energizes us in our witness, that blasts apart the lies of Satan, that gives our personal lives and our organizations their reason for being!

So why do we need a vision at all? Why isn't the Great Commission simply enough? A congregation's vision helps focus attention on the specific ways they will carry out Christ's command in their community. Servant leaders work with followers to craft a compelling vision, knowing it will help provide

- Direction—Vision produces the road map for the organization. Communicating that vision generates excitement about the trip.

- Motivation—It's confusing for followers to try to perform well in a directionless situation.

- Commitment—A clearly understood vision creates commitment—persistence with purpose.

- Inspiration—Vision makes it possible for leaders to "take charge without taking control." With a vision, you can inspire volunteers instead of ordering them.

- Accountability—When a group creates a shared vision and agrees on core values and goals, they design a map of where they want to go as a team. This creates a built-in accountability much more powerful than the traditional supervisor-worker reporting relationship.

- Meaning—Everyone is looking for reasons to do the work they do. In the past, we needed the money to live. Today, more people and more institutions generate more dollars than they absolutely need. Money becomes a crude measure of success, but we're looking for something more.

Perhaps Robert K. Greenleaf puts it best:

> Someone . . . must paint the dream. For anything to happen, there must be a dream. And for anything great to happen, there must be a great dream. [At] the growing edge . . . will be a painter of great dreams for all [the congregation's] people, something to lift their sights above the ordinary

and give them a great goal to strive for—something for each person to strive for. (*Servant Leadership: A Journey into the Nature of Legitimate Power and Greatness,* p. 88)

Paintbrush, anyone?

Teams, Trust, and Vision

The organizational vision motivates, inspires, and gives meaning to the lives of individuals, even as it creates accountability and sets direction. A clearly communicated vision also enhances the overall functioning of the organization by forging unity, aligning individual efforts, and building confidence in followers. We turn to look at these benefits briefly now.

In the first place, a clearly articulated vision helps to forge unity; it bonds a team together. This happened little by little as I interacted with the evangelism visitation team I described at the beginning of this chapter. Our common concern for the eternal welfare of the people in our neighborhood drew us together. By way of contrast, perhaps you've experienced life on a team that had no shared vision. Almost always, people begin to question one another's motives. Members wonder whether others will act out of selfish motives or in the interests of the organization. In such a situation, trust is highly unlikely. Serving on teams like that is usually quite uncomfortable.

Second, a team vision helps align the efforts of individual team members. It creates coordination. This is especially important for teams with interdependent tasks. Let's take a VBS-planning team as an example. One person may be charged with overseeing the physical arrangements (facilities, snacks, equipment). A second volunteer organizes teacher recruitment and training. A third may coordinate visitor follow-up. If these three people are energized and guided by a common goal—outreach to neighborhood children and their families—their efforts will come together more easily.

- The facilities director will plan for numbers of students that exceed (perhaps by far) current Sunday school enrollment.

- If he rents a tent for holding classes, he may arrange to keep it set up on the lawn for a family reception after the next Sunday's service so teachers can meet visiting families.

- The recruiter will plan to invite teachers to stick around for the reception and will make sure that most of them can do so.

- The follow-up coordinator will want to be on hand that particular Sunday morning too and may volunteer to have her follow-up volunteers bake cookies for the reception.

What if the only goal is to hold VBS? The facilities coordinator may not think to provide the extra classroom space a tent would offer. The recruiter may organize only enough teachers to accommodate the congregation's own children. The follow-up coordinator may not show up at the VBS reception at all, believing her job doesn't start until the VBS program has concluded. Few of the visiting students or their parents will recognize the follow-up team members who visit them in their homes after VBS. Because of this, the witnessing potential may be quite limited.

These are the differences in coordination and results that a clear, common, specific, and meaningful vision can make!

Unity. Alignment. Confidence. According to David Atwater and Bernard Bass in their article "Transformational Leadership in Teams," research has shown that an inspirational vision encourages followers to set higher goals for themselves, to aspire to greater accomplishment. In the church this can work in even more powerful ways, I believe, because we realize we are not limited by our own capacity or potential. God is able to do even more than we can ask or imagine. And He is at work through us and in us (Ephesians 3:20). What confidence this gives us in our praying and in our working—all to bring Him honor!

All of these benefits can come about, though, only as the leader gives the team a clear and accurate understanding of the vision, the task, and the part each person plays in making the vision a reality. If the leader has already established relationships of trust with the individuals and with the team, communicating the vision and establishing team buy-in become much easier.

Vision—Fragmented or Holistic?

Maybe by now you're asking yourself a larger question about vision in the local congregation. Does the vision belong to the whole church? Or does each organization have its own? If the VBS team has a vision and the evangelism visitation team has a second, separate vision, where's the unity? If you have 12 different groups, teams, and committees in your congregation, won't you end up with a splintered approach to ministry?

These questions and others like them raise valid concerns. Those responsible for setting the congregation's overall direction and emphasis—the pastor and perhaps the elders or deacons—must care deeply about this issue. Most organizational experts agree that each team's mission or purpose must align with the overall organizational vision—its mission.

This implies, of course, that the congregation has in fact developed such a vision or mission statement and continually communicates it in a compelling way. The congregation's mission, then, keeps each individual committee, team, or auxiliary organization from pulling at cross purposes.

In a sense, the overarching congregational mission creates and supports what several business experts call "a covenantal relationship" between and among members and the various subgroups in the congregation (see, for example, Bennis's *On Becoming a Leader* and DePree's "The Leader's Legacy"). Based on a shared commitment to common ideals, common values, and common goals, a congregational mission statement makes it possible for each member to find fulfillment and meaning as he or she prays and works toward the fulfillment of the mutual vision.

Such a covenantal, overarching vision statement helps ensure that the organization is "clear at its core," as Margaret Wheatley puts it. This, in turn, makes it possible for individuals and groups to create, in Wheatley's words, "a plurality of effective solutions" to problems and challenges that arise. It unleashes members' creativity. What makes this so powerful is the fact that each of the solutions will express what Wheatley calls a "deeper coherence"; the solutions will reflect an understanding of what the organization is working to become. Subgroups will not spin off wildly in all directions, but will instead come together in synergy, in system-wide coherence.

The pastor plays a key role here, particularly as he verbalizes and embodies the overarching vision. In addition, he can champion the specific missions and projects of the various congregational teams, reminding everyone in an inspirational way of the importance of each team's success to the overall mission of the congregation.

Does Vision Matter That Much? Really?

In a word, yes. Richard Kovaceirch, CEO of Norwest, the enormously successful financial services company, once told the *Wall Street Journal*, "I could leave our strategic plan on a plane . . . and it wouldn't make any difference" (quoted in Pfeffer, "The Real Keys to High Performance," online article). That's not to put down strategic planning. Kovacevich's comment emphasizes the enormous power of a well-conceived, meaningful, compelling vision statement. Acting in line with that kind of vision, members can go a long way down the road toward achieving organizational goals—on their own.[5]

As we conclude this chapter, we turn to some specific guidelines for servant leaders who want to interweave vision and trust to form a tapestry of meaning and significance in their organizations as they interact with their followers.

First, servant leaders articulate a clear and appealing vision. You may strengthen an existing one or create a new one, but look for dozens of ways to communicate it. Repeat it again and again, in authentic—not gimmicky—ways. Display it on a plaque in the narthex. Paint it on your church van. Print cards for every member. Recite it at the beginning of each meeting. Comment on it when that's appropriate in the sermon or in each monthly newsletter. Above all, use it as a living, breathing guide for action, as a measure for evaluating decision alternatives.

Second, keep on explaining how your group can achieve its vision. Convince them that, though the vision is challenging, it is feasible. Don't pretend to know all the answers about implementation. Say things such as, "I wish I understood all the strategic ins and outs, but with everyone's best thinking, and especially with our Lord's guidance, I'm sure we can find a way to do it."

Third, use a straightforward, uncomplicated strategy. Scholars who study transformational leadership, a theory similar to servant leadership, have found evidence that an unconventional strategy may work best. But remember to act out of your core identity. If you aim for the merely clever rather than for the authentic, followers will likely see your actions as faddish or as a quick-fix. Instead of implementing it, they may wait around to see when you'll come to your senses.

Fourth, act confidently yourself and express genuine trust in the Lord and in His power and wisdom at work in your followers. Emphasize the positive, and refuse to dwell on obstacles. Help your group remind one another of all the Lord has done in and through your congregation in the past. Keep hope alive for the future!

Fifth, plan ways to help the group take small initial steps toward the goal. Be sure these steps are achievable. Then celebrate the early successes the Lord gives.[6]

Sixth, pay attention to what counts. Budgets and attendance figures don't always (or even often) reflect what the Lord may be doing with, through, and for your team. Instead, why not choose a performance measure related to your vision? For example, some organizations measure

- the percentage of members serving on teams;

- the retention of new members;

- member attitudes;

- the percentage of adults and children in weekly Bible study.

What other creative, vision-based measurements could help you gauge the impact that your efforts, under God's blessing, are making? Remember the business adage "What gets measured gets done."

Finally, lead by example. Model the behaviors you'd like to see in followers. This proves especially true for difficult or unpleasant tasks. During the summer in my high school years I usually helped teach VBS in my home congregation. I'll never forget that the pastor taught a class alongside the rest of us. He always took the toughest class—usually the one with the most difficult discipline problems. And he insisted on taking the most cramped, least pleasant classroom. The rest of the staff jokingly referred to that classroom as "the den of terrors." But he taught with such commitment and joy, I still remember it today—35 years later. That's servant leadership.

Where We've Been and Where We're Headed

Leaders of Great Groups generate and sustain trust by providing direction and meaning. Servant leaders remind their people of what's important and why their work makes a difference. A clear and compelling goal energizes Great Groups and helps them ride out the turbulence of dissent and setbacks. Always, though, the overarching mission of the congregation must guide and frame the mission/vision of the teams, committees, and auxiliary organizations that represent subsets of the congregation as a whole.

Specific techniques and approaches can help leaders build a vision into a congregation's core culture, but, as always, servant leaders choose behaviors congruent with their own core identity and values. This ensures authenticity and guards against leadership by gimmick.

In the next chapter we will explore ways to build and empower teams, ways that really work. Even among business leaders, one often hears complaints such as

"We don't have teams. What we really have are staff meetings."

How can servant leaders avoid similar nonproductive approaches to group effort while building high-trust teams? Let's take a look!

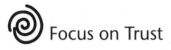 Focus on Trust

1. Tell about a Great Group you once belonged to. What was your group's vision? What obstacles did you face? What made your group great? How would you describe the level of trust in that group? How did it develop?

2. Why might a congregation name survival as one of its top goals? From what you've seen in the Scriptures and in this chapter, why might having survival as a goal prove counterproductive? Suppose you served as a consultant to a survival-focused congregation. How might you approach your task? Why would addressing the issue of trust be crucial?

3. What factors sometimes make it hard for leaders in the church to "think big and think new"? (Consider issues of trust as you answer.) How and why might Satan be involved in opposition to "big and new"? What does this say to church leaders as they strategize?

4. How should each congregational team's vision fit in

with the overarching corporate vision of the congregation? Why?

5. What performance measures does your congregation use? What additions or changes might help you more accurately capture what our Lord is doing in and through your congregation?

4

Your End of the Boat

Parents welcomed the idea. Or most did. Tuition at the parish school forced most church families to dig deep, very deep, into their pockets. The school board proposed uniforms as a way to ease the clothing budget for families.

A sample uniform hung in the principal's office for a month or so toward the end of the school year to give families plenty of time to examine, find, and buy the regulation shirts, skirts, shorts, and trousers. Toward the middle of May, one parent ran into a sale at a local department store. She phoned her friends and, before long, several dozen families had snapped up enough pieces to outfit their children.

Then, the last week of school, the uniform disappeared from the school office. When parents asked the principal about it, he looked sheepish and tap-danced around the issue. Finally, a disgusted parent tracked down the chairperson of the board for parish education. "I killed it," he said simply.

"You killed it," the parent retorted. "What about the rest of the board?"

"I mean, we decided against it," said the chair.

Teams and Power

Teams can run amok. This prospect can give servant leaders nightmares. When leaders empower teams but then fail to trust them, teams can't do the organization very much good. Organizations then have, as the last chapter pointed out, not real teams but simply staff meetings, committee meetings. On the other hand, when organizations do empower teams—and mean it—they run the risk that someone on the team or the entire team itself will abuse its power. The board chairperson you met in this chapter's opening story is but one example.

How can teams truly function for the good of the organization? What can leaders—particularly pastors and other professional church staff—do to help keep teams on track? How can trust and empowerment create synergy on congregational teams for the good of the congregation and the kingdom of Christ? Let's look at these issues now.

With or For?

Dwight Eisenhower once said, "It is better to have one person working with you, than to have three people working for you." The idea "we're in this together" energizes team members. It creates synergy, particularly when the team rallies around a common, compelling purpose. At the heart of every Great Group, Warren Bennis proposes, is a shared dream:

> All Great Groups believe they are on a mission from God, that they [can] change the world, make a dent in the universe. It becomes not a job, but a fervent quest. That belief is what brings the necessary cohesion and energy to their work. ("The Secrets of Great Groups," online article)

Chapter 3 developed this idea of vision and its importance in some detail. The first step in moving an organization's vision from dream to reality involves finding gifted people to work together toward the vision. Here immediately the need for trust arises:

> When given a choice, people will choose not to work in a suspicious, distrusting environment. If we want to attract talented people who can handle empowerment successfully, we need to create a high-trust culture. (Shaw, p. 9)

How likely is it that people will line up to serve on the board of parish education with the chairperson you met earlier? Even if congregations create teams and intend to empower them, nothing will happen if power is abused. Such abuse smothers the development of trust.

Power and Purpose

Congregations are not alone in confronting these kinds of problems. Writing in the *Journal of Product Innovation Management*, E. F. McDonough notes that the majority of for-profit firms are having trouble getting teams to live up to their full potential. Margaret Wheatley thinks this failure stems from the fact that many managers grew up believing the best way to manage for excellence was to tell people exactly what to do and then make sure they did it. Control-centered mechanisms can sprout up in Christian organizations as well as for-profit firms. A friend responsible for team building in his company tells of one particularly frustrating congregational meeting. After nearly two hours of fruitless discussion, he stood to his feet and asked pointedly, "Are we here to follow Robert's Rules of Order or to do something worthwhile for the Lord?"

Often fear leads groups or leaders to emphasize strict adherence to formal rules. Fear likely holds some sway in my friend's congregation. Fear leads people to crave prediction and control—the kind of control legalism seems to offer. But in tightly controlled, fear-based environments, leaders must carry the burden of providing everything their machinelike groups cannot—vision, inspiration, intelligence, and courage. Quite a responsibility! Such leaders can also easily wind up carrying most of the workload themselves. No wonder Robert K.

Greenleaf calls power "the central issue of trust." Remember our third key servant-leadership value:

Servant leaders value the freedom and dignity of the individual. Therefore, servant leaders rely primarily on the art of persuasion to create consensus and a sense of community, instead of trying to force compliance by coercion.

Servant leaders need to help the organizations deal with power in new ways, using methods other than command-and-control or coercion. In his book *Leadership*, James McGregor Burns suggests that transformational leadership[7] involves a process wherein leaders and followers build a mutual commitment to organizational objectives and leaders empower followers to achieve these objectives. Terrie Temkin calls this an "atmosphere of mutual influence."

As we saw in the last chapter, leaders go first when it come to developing mutual trust and respect in organizations. Leaders make themselves vulnerable by trusting others first, by openly sharing information about themselves and their motives, by giving others the access needed to develop familiarity, and by listening to followers' ideas and challenges. Jack Lowe, CEO of TDIndustries, adds that in communities built around the servant leadership paradigm, followers trust leaders to listen to their thoughts and ideas. Also, in such communities, leaders trust the judgment of followers.

In high-trust cultures leaders pay special attention to the virtue of transparency. Suspicion will develop if followers begin to believe their leaders habitually share different information with different groups. In high-trust cultures, what you see is what you get. Hidden agendas and political posturing are challenged and eliminated. Overall, the sense that everyone deals with issues up front creates healthy trust.

Think back to the school uniform incident. The parents' inability to find out about the changed uniform policy and the apparently dictatorial approach the board chairperson took would damage trust in most organizations, even if solid reasons lay behind the decision. The lack of transparency, the unilateral use of power by the chairperson, and the principal's apparent failure to confront either of these issues head-on—all would feed the engine of suspicion and mistrust. In this instance, coercion has replaced the processes of consensus and community building.

Leaders Enable Others to Act

Without followers, leaders can accomplish little. Paradoxically, the more a servant leader shares power by giving it away, by delegating it to others, the more power and influence that leader gains! James Kouzes and Barry Posner put the paradox this way:

Leaders enable others to act. They foster collaboration and build spirited teams. They actively involve others. Leaders understand that mutual respect sustains extraordinary efforts; they strive to create an atmosphere of trust and human dignity. They strengthen others by sharing information and providing choice. They give their own power away, making each person capable and powerful. (p. 318)

Why do servant leaders give their own power away? To make it possible for the organization to achieve the vision. Power becomes one of the means to a desired end—a tool, if you will, that leaders wield, lend, share, give, and surrender to advance the group's agenda. Clearly, for servant leaders the focus must lie on the goal, on the vision, not on the privileges or the power of position.

As servant leaders empower people to achieve the vision, they delegate their authority to those followers who most need it to complete the tasks at hand. This requires judgment, an exercise of power in itself! Servant leaders also encourage initiative, and they support followers who show it. Servant leaders allow followers high latitude of discretion. Finally, in empowering followers, servant leaders see to it that followers have the resources they need—funds, people, information, guidelines, and training.

Even when delegating authority, though, leaders act as what Bennis calls "catalytic completers." They take on the roles the team needs: cajoler, taskmaster, protector, doer, or whatever serves to achieve the team's goal.

In all these ways servant leaders empower followers and, in doing so, create a reservoir of trust, a pool of "collaborative capital" the group can use to great advantage.

Multiplying Results

"None of us is as smart as all of us"—so goes the old saying. This adage expresses a truth organizational scholars call "nonsummativity" or "the assembly effect." Groups that collaborate to solve complex problems devise more creative, more workable solutions than any individual working alone. Ann McGee-Cooper, internationally recognized researcher in innovative business approaches, describes it this way:

> It is fascinating to discover that within teams who know how to dialogue, creating richer shared meaning, collective intelligence rises to become much higher than the brightest member of the team.

But note the contrast:

> However, in teams where individuals compete to be right and have the last [word], the collective intelligence falls below the level of the least bright

> team member because the brighter members begin
> to cancel each other out with power plays and
> intimidation. Others duck and choose not to sur-
> face their insights because it is not safe to do so.
> (pp. 82–83)

When did you last attend a meeting like that? Few people enjoy such an exercise. However, the good news is that self-managed teams can be far more productive than any other form of organizing. Research has shown a clear correlation between participating and productivity. In for-profit organizations, productivity in truly self-managed environments is at a minimum 35 percent higher than in traditional, command-and-control organizations! How does this happen? Charles Cadwell, an expert on managing teams, proposes the following:

- Teams accomplish more with less waste. They can make the best use of each member's talents and skills. Higher-performance teams let each member do what he/she does best or most comfortably.

- Teams produce higher quality work. When everyone buys into the goal, team members spur one another on to greater heights.

- Team members often stretch one another to develop new skills. They learn from one another and model for one another new ways of doing things.

- Team members are often happier. People who

enjoy what they are doing and who believe they are making a contribution are often willing to do more.

Kouzes and Posner add another advantage that teams bring their parent organizations: Teams provide a social support network for their members. Co-workers who support one another are less susceptible to service burnout than workers who have no such support system. Supportive team relationships help maintain both personal and organizational vitality. Bennis notes that supportive team relationships also help generate the courage that commitment requires.

The Church Council— A Multidisciplinary Team

Let's bring this theory back to earth now as we discuss a multidisciplinary team quite common in congregations—the church council. I consider it multidisciplinary, because those who sit on the council in most churches each represent a different point of view, if not always a different skill set.

At St. Timothy congregation, for example,

- the head elder brings a special concern for the overall spiritual well-being of members;

- the chairperson of the board of Christian education brings a concern for the various educational agencies of the parish—the Sunday school, VBS, perhaps the day school, and so on;

- the chairperson of the stewardship committee represents a concern for members' maturity in the wise use of God's gifts to individual members;

- the treasurer—who pays the bills—needs to make sure that the congregation lives within its means.

On it goes around the table when the St. Timothy church council meets—the boards of missions, evangelism, building and grounds, and perhaps a few members-at-large. The pastor, charged by Christ and responsible to Him, carries into council meetings the overarching concerns of shepherding individuals (1 Peter 5:1–4), managing the household of God (Ephesians 2:19–22), and carrying out the Great Commission (Matthew 28:18–20).

The church council at St. Timothy needs a clear understanding of the congregation's vision for ministry. It needs a firm commitment to that vision as the congregation's Spirit-led response to the Gospel. The members need to trust one another, and they need the freedom to deal with issues head-on in a mature and honest way. What else do they need?

1. Members of the team need to be competent. Collaboration by incompetents will not succeed, no matter how well-meaning the individuals are. In addition, the members need to recognize that they each bring different skills to the table. They each con-

sider issues from different viewpoints. They need to respect one another's expertise and value the wisdom their collective diversity creates.

2. The group needs consensus on the processes they will use to explore problems and come to decisions. Team processes should be transparent to such a degree that everyone understands the procedures and rules.

3. Individual group members need strong interpersonal skills. I once served on a church council in which two or three strong—and pessimistic—personalities dominated. Neither the chair nor the pastor wanted to confront the destructive behavior. One by one, individuals dropped off the council. They all had other reasons, but most admitted privately that discomfort with unresolved conflicts and just plain rude behavior on the part of a few members of the council lay at the root of the dropout problem.

4. All group members need to show mutual tolerance and respect. They do not need to be best friends, but everyone must be willing to focus on managing one another's strengths rather than chafing at one another's quirks and idiosyncrasies.

5. Groups need good information and ways to accurately update that information. This, in turn, points us back to the importance of good commu-

nication skills and effective communication chan-
nels.

6. Church groups need support from the pastor and
from the elders or deacons—the people we might
call the congregation's top management team.

7. High-performance teams also need ample recognition for their efforts. Congregations need to learn
and use many alternative ways to say thank you.

8. Finally, teams need a process by which they take
stock on a regular, consistent basis. The members
need to ask one another, "How are we doing? How
could we do even better?" Remember, it's possible
to be so forward-looking that we forget to evaluate
progress toward our goals.

Cohesion in Teams

From the time of the earliest studies of organizational behavior, researchers have seen the importance of
two dynamics:

- the task dimension—how the group's work gets
done;

- the interpersonal dimension—how group members
and their leaders interact with one another and the
extent to which they show appreciation and support.

Part of the interpersonal dimension involves group cohesiveness. Cohesiveness is a positive affect (or feeling) among group members that increases their desire to stay in the group. Cohesiveness can be a powerful force for good in groups. Consider these three council members at St. Timothy:

Jim Clark, the recently elected chair of the congregation's board of fellowship, has belonged to St. Timothy for only 22 months. He feels honored to sit on the council in so short a time. As Jim enters the room for his first council meeting, other members go out of their way to help him feel comfortable and welcome. As he listens to the more experienced members speak to issues in the meeting, their wisdom and spiritual maturity impress him. As the meeting ends, Jim is well on his way to internalizing the council's values and viewpoints.

Lynne Parker, an officer in a local bank and treasurer for St. Timothy, has served on the council several different times over the past 15 years. Lynne believes the congregation needs to use sounder business practices in its financial dealings. She has privately butted heads with the council's chairperson over this issue several times in the past few months. In council meetings, though, Lynne is more subdued in her arguments. The group as a whole disagrees with several of Lynne's more radical priorities, and Lynne knows it.

Max Schultz hates formality, but on the night the council meets at St. Timothy, he puts on a tie. Pastor

Wilson has stressed the need for excellence as the council does "the Lord's business," and the council members have bought into this accent. Meeting minutes, board reports, special projects—all the council's work gets done in a professional way. Some members dress more casually than Max, but Max just feels better when he wears a tie.

Jim, Lynne, and Max illustrate some benefits high cohesion creates in groups. In highly cohesive groups, members tend to internalize group norms and values. The group can exert quite a lot of pressure on members' behavior—Lynne's views on finances and Max's personal dress code are two examples. Also, when highly cohesive groups set high standards of performance, members' values and actions will generally reflect this.

What creates cohesiveness? Donald Ellis and Aubrey Fisher, who have studied organizational communication for decades, propose that groups tend to be most cohesive when

- the group is small;

- membership is stable;

- members interact regularly;

- members share goals;

- members come from similar backgrounds;

- membership is exclusive and limited;

• the group has high status in the organization or the larger society.

Michael Schrage, frequent writer on creative collaboration, notes that many studies have shown that when a group includes more than 12 members, both decision quality and efficiency begin to degrade. Schrage also points out that it's rare for a group with many more than 12 members to enjoy a lively discussion in which everyone participates.

In addition, groups tend to become more cohesive when they perceive an external threat or enemy. This suggests that the St. Timothy council might grow even more cohesive if Pastor Wilson or some other member were to remind the group regularly and meaningfully of Satan's schemes to thwart the spread of the Gospel in the St. Timothy community.

Finally, cohesiveness grows when groups experience success and when they spend a great deal of time together. As you evaluate the cohesiveness of your own group or congregation, however, consider the fact that high cohesiveness may or may not be a good thing. The reason has to do with a phenomenon called "groupthink."

The Pitfalls of Cohesiveness

Suppose Lynne Parker is right about the shaky financial position St. Timothy faces. In fact, suppose she has understated the problem, even in her fairly frank discussions with the pastor and the council's chairperson. The other members may, because of the pressure they place on Lynne, get her to stop talking about the danger altogether. It's even possible that, over time, they will get Lynne to change her interpretation of reality!

But if Lynne's original interpretation is correct, in time this aspect of the council's cohesiveness could threaten the congregation's well-being, perhaps even its existence. A degree of cohesiveness high enough to expose the group to this kind of danger is called "groupthink."

Groupthink led to the Challenger disaster in which seven astronauts lost their lives. Groupthink also helped to create the Bay of Pigs fiasco during the Kennedy administration. In both cases, competent experts found their better judgment overridden by the pressure to conform to the group's will.

What can counter groupthink? One basic remedy needs to be consistently applied: People in groups need leaders who can help them understand that the conflict of ideas is healthy and necessary, while conflict between individuals is unhealthy and unnecessary.

This is easy to say and hard to do, particularly in congregational groups where individuals often tend to equate Christian love with being agreeable—going along to get along. We can also tie ideas too closely to individuals and thus take questions and critiques too personally. Servant leaders consequently need to teach and model healthy conflict for groups. Another technique that can work well involves assigning a group member to play "devil's advocate" at each meeting. That member's job is to pinpoint weaknesses in the suggestions and proposals the group makes. It's best to rotate this assignment so as not to burden any one person with a task—and perhaps eventually a reputation—many people would consider negative. Bennis writes: "Leaders encourage dissent and diversity in the pursuit of a shared vision and understand the difference between healthy, creative dissent and self-serving obstructionism."

Where We've Been and Where We're Headed

In a canoe, no one can say to his companions, "Your end of the boat is sinking." Similarly, teams float or sink together. Skilled, multidisciplinary teams work together to attain common goals. Together, people collaborating toward common goals have enormous potential! Congregations thinking about leveraging the power of teams may find the suggestions below helpful. The checklist reflects many of the main points this chapter has highlighted:

1. Be certain teams make sense for your organization.

2. Start small; perhaps you can experiment with one

or two teams as you begin.

3. Train everyone involved. It's especially important that each team member understands the small-group communication process and has adequate conflict resolution skills.

4. Give the team a clear and compelling purpose; make sure each team member buys in.

5. State clear expectations. Sometimes it helps to go around the table as the meeting begins, giving everyone a chance to unload whatever is on his or her mind. This often diffuses hidden agendas.

6. Establish the role of team leaders.

7. Establish the role of "coaches"—outside consultants who can step in to help if glitches arise in the group process.

8. Know when to step in if you are needed and when to let the group continue to wrestle with a problem or resolve a crisis on their own. If the pastor or other congregation authorities step in too soon, it will likely be perceived as interference and will demotivate the group.

9. Give teams a lot of feedback.

10. Trust the team to make important decisions.

11. Encourage the team and publicly recognize and celebrate its accomplishments.

12. Decide if it works.

We turn next to the issue of stewardship, trust, and servant leadership. How do leaders keep teams and the individuals in them motivated to use and to develop their unique gifts and abilities? How do servant leaders allow for individual differences while still getting things done through groups? What styles of leadership work best with specific teams, and how does the servant leader decide which style of leadership to use? These questions and their answers all grow from one of the most powerful servant-leader values—stewardship of followers' God-given abilities.

◎ Focus on Trust

1. Explain the quote from Dwight Eisenhower, "It's better to have one person working with you, than to have three people working for you."

2. How can a compelling organizational purpose replace the need for coercion on the part of leaders? How does such a purpose impact trust?

3. Why would leaders find empowered teams an attractive alternative to staff meetings? What reservations might leaders have? What reservations might followers have? What reservations do you personally have? How would you answer each of these sets of reservations?

4. How might you prevent the negative effects of groupthink in the team(s) you are responsible for without losing the benefits of healthy cohesiveness? Outline a long-term strategy.

5. Analyze Jesus' processes of influencing followers. Consider any examples of coercive power He wielded. Also consider His approach to community building and consensus. How did He bring His followers along? How well did it work? What did you learn about trust from your analysis?

5

I Am a Human Being— Do Not Fold, Spindle, or Mutilate!

They should have celebrated. The army had just put down a rebellion that had threatened to bring down King David's reign. Yet celebration was the last thing on David's mind. Instead, he cloistered himself in a small room above the city gate to grieve over his dead son— his seditious and rebellious son, Absalom.

David might have lost his throne despite his army's victory that day. But Joab, David's general, intervened. "See here," Joab in essence told David in 2 Samuel 19:1–8. "You are disgracing your loyal followers. They saved your life today. And your family. Get out there and thank them, or you'll turn this victory into the worst defeat of your life. You owe your people thanks!"

What Leaders Owe Their Followers

Perhaps you are used to thinking in terms of what followers owe their leaders. Scripture describes much of that in detail.[8] Even though perhaps we aren't so used to

70

thinking about what leaders owe their followers in the church, Scripture also supports this notion. The account of Joab's counsel in 2 Samuel 19 gives but one example. The New Testament also points to the duties of spiritual leaders in the areas of

- pure doctrine (1 Timothy 1:3–7; 4:16);

- setting a good example (1 Timothy 3:2, 7; 4:12);

- hospitality (1 Timothy 3:2);

- a good-natured demeanor (1 Timothy 3:3);

- humility (1 Timothy 3:16);

- reverence (1 Timothy 3:8);

- honesty (1 Timothy 3:8);

- good stewardship of one's spiritual gifts (1 Timothy 4:14);

- consistent, persistent, diligent work (1 Timothy 5:17).

Scripture lists and illustrates additional expectations as well. Max DePree suggests four basic duties all leaders owe their followers. Do you see these exemplified any-where in Scripture? Are any of the four important in the church's leaders today?

- Respect in the understanding that "I cannot do much without you."

- A perceivable level of fairness, especially in "promises made, promises kept."

- Direction and vision toward creating hope in a brighter tomorrow.

- Productive conversations about the gifts the follower brings to the organization and the kind of contributions the follower wishes to make.

DePree contends that the leader's concern about best using and developing followers' gifts helps to create hope in followers' hearts. Charles Handy would agree, adding the fact that each person is uniquely gifted and thus has a unique contribution to make:

> I do believe that we are each of us unique. We each—institutions as well as individuals—have something to contribute to the world, and the search for meaning is finding out what that is before we die. ("The Search for Meaning," online article)

This emphasis on unique giftedness and the meaning that comes from contributing to others based on one's gifts intersects with the fourth servant-leadership value:

> Servant leaders want each follower fully to develop his or her individual gifts and abilities. Thus, servant leaders seek to steward follower giftedness, appreciating and empowering followers to develop and use their abilities to their maximum potential. Servant leaders take the risks inherent in empowering others, because they know that it ultimately

strengthens organizations and brings the joy of
fulfillment to the individual.

The old adage "People are our most important asset"
is actually true. Jeffrey Pfeffer, professor of organization
behavior at Stanford University, points to research that
shows organizational success in the for-profit sector
depends more on effectively developing people and
their gifts than on large size, on operating in a high
growth industry, or on becoming lean and mean
through downsizing!

What does this say to the church? For one thing, we
need not grow to the size of the mega-church up the
street before we can claim to carry out our Lord's mission.[9] What matters much more than size is stewarding
the giftedness God has given each person in our particular congregation. Speaking of secular organizations,
DePree writes, "For years we have underestimated people." Have we in the church done that too? Has your
congregation done it?

Servant leaders believe that everyone has the potential to be a strong contributor in the organization. Still,
leaders who see followers only as means to an end
destroy trust. They undermine the values of any organization that believes in respect for the individual—the
church included.

More Than Means to an End

Whether one leads staff employed by the organization or volunteers who donate their time to the organization, workers do their best only in a nurturing, valuing environment. Only that kind of environment allows people to trust, create, risk, and measure up to the expectations of others. In addition, only that kind of environment helps them to grow in their abilities.

In contrast, when leaders do not recognize the worth of their followers and celebrate followers' contributions, followers become angry and often shameful. Joab pointed to the dangers of such an emotional powder keg long ago in his conversation with King David, didn't he? The desire for recognition is "an extraordinarily powerful part of the human psyche" (Shaw, p. 92).

Henry Mintzberg, who has devoted his career to the study of effective leadership, writes about "quiet management" in this regard. This kind of leadership is about thoughtfulness rooted in experience:

> Words like wisdom, trust, dedication, and judgment apply. Leadership works because it is legitimate, meaning that it is an integral part of the organization and so has the respect of everyone there. Tomorrow is appreciated because yesterday is honored. That makes today a pleasure. ("Managing Quietly," online article)

Two important concepts emerge from Mintzberg's brief paragraph—the importance of acknowledging yesterday's contribution and the importance of leadership in the organizational process. In each case, people must become much more than merely means to a desired end.

Acknowledging Yesterday

Leaders acknowledge the contribution the organization's people made yesterday. This "yesterday" includes all 20 or 50 or 150 years that the Lord has, in His grace, granted to your organization. As I note in *Servant Leadership: Setting Leaders Free,* part of stewarding our organizations involves acknowledging and building on the legacy we have inherited from those who have gone before us.

God has given me the privilege of working at Concordia Publishing House (CPH). During my tenure here, the "House," as employees call it, celebrated its 125th anniversary. Each day as I leave the building, I walk past a trophy case of sorts. Inside a frame that measures about four feet square, visitors and employees alike see photos of 50-year CPH veterans. Most of these 32 people now reside in heaven, but all have given five decades or more of their earthly lives to serving Christ by publishing resources to encourage, inform, and strengthen His people. What a heritage! I'm glad we honor it! What does your congregation or organization do to honor its heritage, particularly its people heritage?

"Yesterday" need not stretch so far into the past. It's just as important to ask, "How do we recognize and appreciate those who served faithfully last week, last month, or last year?" A culture of appreciation creates trust and motivates people in the present to work toward contributing their best efforts today and tomorrow. In this way, the gifts and abilities of individuals grow and blossom for the good of the entire group. How often does your congregation say thank you?

- Do you honor the VBS staff in January when you have your Sunday school volunteer banquet?

- Do you post photos of the youth-group car wash, showing plenty of pictures of the adult leaders as well as student participants?

- Does the pastor write a brief, personal note or e-mail to each member on his/her birthday, expressing thanks to God for that person and his/her volunteer efforts during the year?

- Does appreciation prevail in the culture of the congregation in informal ways? Do leaders model it? For instance, does Joe Elder stop Sally Sunday after worship to thank her for teaching the preschool class? Does Joe do this in front of Sally's husband, sister, or best friend or in front of one of the preschool children's parents?

- Does the congregation's time of public prayer include requests that the Lord send the workers you need for various specific programs? Does the time of prayer in the worship service regularly include thanksgiving for specific people and their efforts on behalf of the congregation's mission? Such prayers are *not* a manipulative ploy to recruit volunteers! Rather, they recognize the Holy Spirit's essential role in motivating volunteers and the gift-edness God alone gives for serving His people!

These examples all illustrate Mintzberg's first concern for quiet management—the importance of leaders' acknowledging yesterday and the contributions followers have made. Mintzberg's second concern for quiet management involves the importance of leadership.

Leadership vs. Empowerment?

All of the talk about empowerment can make leaders nervous. From a nonservant perspective, professional managers sometimes fear that "self-directed work teams" (SDWT) will lead to layoffs—their own! In contrast, experienced servant leaders understand that work groups cannot prosper without leadership. The responsibilities of leaders change with the advent of SDWTs, but those responsibilities by no means disappear. Read the description of empowerment that Kimball Fisher gives below. Fisher is cofounder of the Fisher Group and an internationally recognized authority on high-performance work systems. As you read, look for issues of stewardship, of the role leaders fill in recognizing and stimulating the growth of followers in their areas of gift-edness:

> What is empowerment? It is a function of four variables: authority, resources, information, and accountability. You might remember these variables by using the [mnemonic device] ARIA, which is composed of the first letter of each variable. The beauty of the opera solo of the same name depends on whether the music is written, performed, and accompanied well. Similarly, the empowerment melody works only when all the variables are in complete harmony. To feel empowered, people need formal authority and all the resources (e.g., budget, equipment, time, and training) necessary to do something with the new authority. They also need timely, accurate information to make good decisions. And they need a personal sense of accountability for the work. (p. 11)

Fisher goes on to explain that there are varying degrees of empowerment. Empowerment isn't something you have or you don't have. Rather, it's a continuum. I see this aspect of empowerment as a stewardship issue also. Take, for instance, the Christian growth committee (CGC) at St. John's. When Pastor Harris arrived, he found this group meeting monthly but accomplishing little. He set out to empower the group. While he did not have a step-by-step plan fully fleshed out when he began, this is how his work with the group progressed:

Year 1: The pastor met with the CGC each month, paying particular attention to the devotions he led. In them he laid the groundwork for a basic Law/Gospel understanding of Scripture. He aimed also at helping CGC members understand the Sacraments more fully and treasure them more deeply. He also shared his goals for Christian education in the congregation, especially as those involved helping adults grow in faith. He worked at listening to individual members of the CGC—why they had joined the group, what their interests were, what their own faith journey had been like, what their hopes and dreams for the congregation involved, and so on. Likewise, he shared his hopes and dreams and his love for Jesus with the group.

Year 2: Pastor Harris continued to listen to each individual group member as he led the group through a planning process. They surveyed the congregation. They ordered samples of adult Bible study materials. They began to set goals for the adult-nurture process at St. John's. They started whetting the congregation's appetite for growth in the Word through monthly newsletter articles. They began providing resources for individual Bible study and devotional resources. They recruited teachers and developed a brochure. Above all, they prayed together.

Year 3: As the school year began, more adults than ever before attended Bible classes on Sunday morning and throughout the week. (St. John's was also offering more options than ever before!) As the pastor contributed to the discussion, the CGC evaluated the courses they offered and began to suggest additional possibilities. He reserved the right to approve all materials and all teachers, but began to release the reins of control he had held tightly at first. Bob Anderson, who had shown a deepening understanding of God's grace in Christ, began leading CGC devotions. When Phyllis Pfizer suggested that the group expand its vision to include the congregation's youth and young adults, the group collaborated on a revised vision statement.

Year 4: This was the year the pastor saw the group gel into a fully self-directed work team. He occasionally attended the CGC meetings, and he reviewed their plans before they sent publicity pieces out. However, he had come to trust their judgment. The members had come to trust him too, and they felt thankful for the ways he had nurtured their growth in Christ while grooming them for more meaningful service. Dale Johnson put it this way:

> I have an MBA and I serve on several teams at work. But just because I know how things work in business doesn't mean I'm an expert at church. I appreciated the pastor's kindness and encouragement. He was never condescending. And he made

use of what I already know. I know how a SDWT is supposed to function, but I never thought I'd see one at church. I'm more excited than ever about being part of this congregation and growing in my faith and service.

Attention to People

Pastor Harris modeled what Mintzberg calls "quiet management" in a powerful, person-sensitive way. Mintzberg notes:

> Quiet managers strengthen the cultural bonds between people, not by treating them as detachable "human resources" . . . but as respected members of the cohesive social system. When people are trusted [in these ways], they don't have to be empowered. ("Managing Quietly," online article)

Pastor Harris developed trust in the CGC to an extent that it created a dynamic sense of empowerment. Notice, though, that Pastor Harris used massive amounts of any leader's scarcest resource—time and attention. Achieving worthwhile goals demands this kind of investment. There are no shortcuts. Leaders who invest minimal time and effort before entrusting critical congregational functions to SDWTs will likely come away bruised and muttering, "Teams don't work."

Creating, nurturing, and trusting SDWTs is not a gimmick or a quick-fix way to lighten the servant leader's own workload. It involves a deeply held constellation of values—stewardship values. Leaders create a covenant when they help others grow and develop, and that help is reciprocated. People who feel capable of influencing their leaders are more strongly attached to those leaders and more committed to effectively carrying out their responsibilities. They **own** their jobs.

Paying attention to individual followers, to their specific needs, talents, interests, and abilities, paves the way for involving them productively and meaningfully in organizational activities and growth experiences. When musician John Lennon attained fame and fortune, he gave the aunt who raised him a gold plaque. Inscribed on the plaque were her own words, evidently words she repeated often during Lennon's adolescence: "You'll never make a living playing that guitar." Lennon was one of the most influential songwriters of his generation. His aunt, living for years with him in the same home, couldn't see his gift and failed to encourage it.

Whose gifts could you be overlooking today?

Developing Groups

In the Christian growth committee example we looked at, we saw Pastor Harris show individual consideration to each team member. We also saw him treating the team differently as it matured. Servant leaders develop individuals and their gifts. Servant leaders also develop teams, stretching and pulling them toward growth as the team develops. How might a servant leader go about developing church teams in this way?

1. By understanding the team's task and its members' gifts. This enables the leader to allocate tasks to the most appropriate member(s).

2. By accurately assessing whether to use an individual or a team to tackle a given task. For simple tasks, groups perform only as well as the best person in them—and only if they take that person's advice. For simple problems, groups usually also take longer. These factors together lead to the conclusion that for simple problems, a qualified individual should make necessary decisions.[10]

3. By working toward a common set of assumptions about the privileges and duties of members throughout the congregation and in all its teams.

4. By building teams and training them, not throwing them into the water and leaving them to drown.

5. By adjusting the leadership approach or style to the maturity and the needs of the group.

Let's focus in depth on these last two—building teams and using appropriate leadership styles.

Forming Teams

If simple tasks call for attention by individuals, complex tasks are best entrusted to competent groups. To be competent, a group needs members with diverse, relevant skills. They need open, accurate communication, both among themselves and with relevant people and groups outside the team. They also, as we have seen before, need to trust one another.

As leaders assemble a team, they do well to recall that, in general, teams composed of members with higher abilities will outperform members of lower ability. However, there are some interesting and important exceptions to this rule:

- If members of lesser abilities pursue better-than-average team strategies, they can outperform teams with more-gifted members.

- If less-able teams overlearn their task, they can outperform teams with more-gifted members.

- If less-able teams are exceptionally motivated, they can achieve more than a less-motivated team, despite that team's more-gifted members.

As leaders assemble a team, they therefore will want to consider the abilities, experiences, and motivation of potential members. They also do well to match team size to the tasks at hand. We saw in chapter 4 that a team with more than 12 members probably cannot count on eager participation by all members. In addition, organizational research shows that groups with 5 or 6 members have the fullest, most productive discussions. Groups with 8 to 10 members may work best for tasks that need less one-on-one discussion. Overall, groups with between 5 and 10 members seem to make it possible to include a diverse enough combination of views and skills, while still allowing for full participation by each group member.

Leaders may want to add a few more members for particularly large and complex tasks. However, leaders of larger groups need to stay alert for problems in coordination and a potential loss of motivation that seems to plague large groups.

Building Teams

If we want SDWTs to be more than merely staff meetings or committee meetings, we need to invest time and attention in helping them understand their role and grow in the process of working together. The description of Pastor Harris's work with his Christian growth committee only scratched the surface of what he as a servant leader did to nurture the group into a functioning, mature, productive team. As you work with congregational teams—either staff or volunteers—find ways to incorporate these dynamics of team building:

1. Keep coming back to the team's core purpose. You probably cannot communicate the vision too often! Remember, "The leader's job is to keep the projector focused."

2. Use ceremonies and rituals. Group prayer, rites of

installation, gathering around the baptismal font for a devotion centered on the Great Commission, and many other rituals will help your group understand—at a deeply spiritual level—the honor of serving Jesus and the importance of the team's task.

3. Encourage and facilitate social interaction. Meet around a coffee pot. Kick off each New Year with a picnic in January. Hold some strategy sessions in your home instead of at the church building. Go out for bagels after some sessions. Get to know one another on a personal level.

4. Use symbols to develop identification with the group. Provide staff T-shirts for VBS volunteers. Have all members of the church council wear red lanyards for easy identification on Sunday morning. Award Sunday school teacher pins. Design a congregation-member bumper sticker. All these and more help solidify group identification.

5. Keep people informed about group activities and achievements. Bulletin-board photo displays work well. So do newsletters, the Sunday bulletin, and brief announcements before or after Bible classes.

6. Conduct process-analysis sessions. Ask, "How could we work together more productively?" Keep revisiting this issue at frequent intervals.

7. Conduct alignment sessions. Ask, "How are we

meshing our projects with the work of other groups in the church? With the congregation's overall mission? How could we better build on other teams' efforts? How could we invite other teams to collaborate with us?"

8. Foster appreciation for diversity. Teach the group about the pitfalls of groupthink. Thank those who disagree agreeably! Do so out loud so the whole group hears. Remind your group often that conflict of ideas is healthy and necessary, while conflict between individuals is not.

Individual Consideration of Teams

If you think about the groups, teams, committees, and task forces you've led or participated in over the years, you will probably agree that each was different. Different tasks, divergent challenges, disparate member-ship, and the varying lengths of time a group has worked together all affect the ways in which groups approach their tasks. Groups need different things from their leaders at different intervals in their life cycles. Wise leaders adjust their strategies to the needs of the group. For example:

- If your style usually involves a primary emphasis on people and relationships, you may need to adopt a more directive approach with a team that spends excessive time hashing out options and never seems to a make a decision.

- If group members don't yet trust one another, you may need to use a more participative style, involving everyone in group discussions and taking time to establish a common basis for interpersonal relationships.

- When task demands are vague and time is critical, you may need to use a more directive rather than relational style.

The developmental stage of a given team will also influence the approach a servant leader chooses in the effort to steward team time and resources.

A Closing Note on Volunteers

Where would we be in congregations if not for our volunteers! Still, sometimes the interface between the church professionals on staff and volunteer workers doesn't connect teams and individuals as smoothly as everyone would like. While everything in this booklet so far applies to working with both paid staff and volunteers, the last few paragraphs in this chapter apply specifically to volunteer-staff teams and trust.

First, as your organization develops teamwork between volunteers and employees (or the called workers on staff), you need to carefully clarify fuzzy functional areas. Make the clarification process as comfortable for everyone as you can, but move beyond job descriptions. Though you do need job descriptions for everyone, they do not answer questions about important nitty-gritty details. For instance:

- Will the church secretary type our group's minutes? Will she run off our Bible study brochures? Or does each board or team do this task on its own?

- Will a staff member meet with each team each time they gather? Who will lead the opening devotion? The closing prayer?

- How will team decisions be communicated to the church staff? To the congregation?

- Who sets each board's yearly budget? What does that budget include? Who has authority to override budgetary limits?

Second, volunteers should strengthen staff capacity and control, not stretch them thinner. Likewise, volunteers should enhance staff competency rather than challenge it. This means, among other things, that in looking for volunteers, no organization should settle for simply throwing warm bodies into the breach. Do all you can to heighten the status of volunteers, making volunteer service an honor. Then accept and retain only those volunteers whose competence and goodwill will facilitate trust with paid staff members.

Affirm, affirm, affirm your volunteers! Call attention to their efforts. Praise their contributions both in public and in person. Build some dollars into your budget for volunteer recognition. Tailor your recognition to the individual whenever possible. For example:

- If your evangelism board chairperson spends many hours each week updating records and making follow-up phone calls, coffee cup always in hand, give him a bag of gourmet coffee beans for his birthday, together with a thank-you note.

- The couple who volunteer as youth counselors month after month might enjoy a meal at an upscale restaurant after doing fast food with the teens so often.

- The Sunday school teacher who greets her class with a smile each week for 10 years might appreciate a handwritten note of appreciation from the pastor—or from a dozen former students.

Third, servant leaders intentionally seek out volunteers whom they see as potential leaders for the future. They take such people under their wing, creating venues in which their protégés can participate in purposeful activities, test their abilities, display their values, and receive support and coaching from more experienced leaders.

Where We've Been and Where We're Headed

In summary, servant leaders who are individually considerate truly encourage the hearts of their followers. They realize that they need not treat everyone alike. Rather, they strive to ensure that all team members feel as if they are in-group members, no matter how much their taste, style, and opinions diverge from those of the leader. Servant leaders do their best to equip their teams and to reward and recognize cooperative, contributing volunteers. All of this creates and strengthens trust.

People really are an organization's most important asset. While many leaders believe this, all too few act on it. When leaders do voluntarily share power with followers, they demonstrate profound trust and respect for followers. Most often followers reciprocate. Both leaders and followers grow in this kind of atmosphere.

In addition, servant leaders use individual consideration as they choose an appropriate style for dealing with teams. Always, servant leaders care about follower growth in addition to team productivity. In their article "Leaders as Stewards," Bill Adams and Cindy Adams put it this way: "Leadership is not just a job, it's a calling. . . . Leaders are entrusted with the stewardship of influencing, teaching, guiding, and guarding" (p. 8).

Our final chapter also addresses growth in individuals and groups—this time from the perspective of healing, forgiveness, and trust.

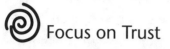 ## Focus on Trust

1. Why do you suppose that for-profit businesses find that developing people and their gifts boosts bottom-line performance? How could such stewardship outperform the advantages of a large organizational size? How could it outperform saving dollars by downsizing? What does this say to leaders in the not-for-profit sector?

2. How does your congregation or organization celebrate your group's "yesterdays"? How could you do this more intentionally and in a way that promotes your mission/vision? How might this impact trust?

3. How do you understand the term empowerment? In what ways do stewardship, servant leadership, trust, and empowerment fit together?

4. Suppose a colleague confides in you that the thought of empowering parishioners makes him very nervous. To what concepts from this chapter might you lead him? How would you hope the conversation might progress?

5. Adams and Adams suggest that leaders ask themselves these questions about their stewardship.

How would you respond?

• How well do I know my people?

• Do they follow me with full hearts and growing trust? How do I know that?

• Will I "go to the wall" for these people, this organization/congregation?

• Do I know my purpose as a leader?

6

Joy in the Journey

Suppose you sat down with the insurance agent who has written the policy on your church property. If she were to ask you to list the congregation's assets, what would you put on the list? The agent would expect to see such things as your building and its furnishings, an inventory of the equipment in the church office, and perhaps the books and the computer in the pastor's study.

I hope that after reading the previous chapter of this book, the chapter about stewarding members' gifts and talents, you will want to list your people among your church's assets too. In addition, you will certainly want to count God's Word and the Sacraments as among your most priceless treasures.

Would you count trust as an organizational asset as well?

Now, of course, no insurance company on earth would insure your congregation against members moving out of your community. And our Lord has guaranteed that hell itself will not steal His means of grace from His church on earth. Along the same lines, certainly no human insurance agent would want to indem-

nify your congregation against a breach of trust—
between individual followers or between those followers
and their leaders.

Even so, suppose that for some reason—such as an
insurance inventory—you had to somehow quantify
the level of trust that exists in your organization right
now. How would you assess this asset? Would you evaluate it as growing, declining, or maintaining a steady
state? On what do you base your answers?

Perhaps by now you no longer find it odd to think
of trust as an organizational asset. Yet before you began
to read, I doubt that you considered trust in those terms.
In their online article "Building and Maintaining Trust:
The Role of Leadership," James Orlikoff and Mary Totten remind us that "trust is a powerful, yet fragile, asset.
It takes years to build a strong, trusting relationship, and
sometimes only a moment to destroy it." Their words
hint at the truth that building trust is a process, a journey rather than a destination.

In this final chapter we will take one last, close look
at that journey. We will explore ways to diagnose the
level of trust in organizations. We will focus on the
process of building trust as a healing process. Finally, we
will tie that healing, trust-building process in with the
processes of listening, empowerment, and team-build-
ing described in earlier chapters.

Caring, Trusting, and Healing

Fran Black's name had appeared by itself on the congregation's ballot for school board chairperson. Thus, no one was surprised when the congregation elected her to serve. The vote was unanimous. With two children enrolled in the parish school, Fran had definite opinions about several changes that could create a better learning atmosphere for students and teachers alike. Fran also had a deep concern about the shallow Christian atmosphere in the school.

Fran had heard about the board members she would inherit. Appointed by the previous chairperson, most had held membership at St. Timothy for only a few years. Long-time members secretly suspected these parents had joined the congregation only to benefit from the lowered tuition payments member families enjoyed. Fran half-believed these rumors, but decided it didn't matter. As the elected chairperson, she marched into her first meeting with a clear mandate to implement several new policies immediately.

Or so Fran thought. The first meeting turned into a "fiasco," to quote Fran the morning after. The second meeting repeated the pain of the first, as did the third. Angry words ricocheted around the meeting room like bullets from a machine gun. No one could agree on anything.

As the fourth meeting drew to a fiery close, Fran began to consider asking all the current board members to step down. That way she could appoint her own board and stock it with friends she knew she could trust. When Fran shared this option with her pastor, he gave her a long look over the frame of his reading glasses. "My dear sister, you need more patience!" he advised. Fran snorted and stalked out of his office.

Commenting on situations not too unlike Fran's, Mintzberg writes:

> Quiet managers care for their organizations; they do not slice away problems as surgeons do. They spend more time preventing problems than fixing them, because they know enough to know when and how to intervene. . . . [It] is like the best of nursing: gentle care that, in itself, becomes cure. ("Managing Quietly," online article)

Those who have stood in Fran's shoes have undoubtedly felt Fran's frustration. But from a servant-leadership standpoint, Fran has come at the organizational tumor with a ruthless scalpel. Her actions will more likely spread the cancer of distrust than eliminate it. Or, to move back to the financial metaphor with which this chapter began, many factors have depleted the asset of trust among school board members at St. Timothy. Rather than making trust deposits, Fran has instead made several more withdrawals.

While acting in good faith, Fran has failed to understand the dynamic of trust. She has failed to see her group's need for healing. In doing so, she has overlooked one of the most important servant-leader values and one of the most important roles servant leaders play:

> Servant leaders value wholeness and growth and want these for their followers and themselves. Thus, they value confession and absolution as a treasure Christ has given to the church. They esteem healing and learning as beneficial and necessary gifts of God in Christ. They model these in their own lives, and they find ways to engage their organizations and followers in the processes of healing and growth as well.

Diagnosing Deficits of Trust

As we begin a discussion of ways to make congregations and other Christian organizations safer, ways to make them places of deeper trust and greater openness, we must first acknowledge that trust is not always wise. Nor is it always possible. Distrust allows people to guard against the less-than-honorable motives of others and the destructive actions by which others could inflict serious harm on us or on our organizations. A friend once told me, "If we try to live in the church on earth as if it were the church in heaven, we leave ourselves open to deep disappointment and unnecessary damage."

Interestingly, Scripture never commands believers to trust one another. It tells us to trust God. It shows us our Lord's total trustworthiness, chiefly by proclaiming Christ crucified and risen for our sins. As a matter of fact, in some situations Scripture urges God's people not to trust human beings—not even ourselves—for things like salvation, true security, peace, and strength (e.g., Psalm 118:8–9; 2 Corinthians 1:9).

Even so, I would contend that many of the commands God gives us in His written Word, together with the Law He has written on human hearts (Romans 2:14–15), serve to evoke behaviors that make trust between people possible. Even passive distrust can cripple relationships. In low-trust organizations, even those people who usually lean toward trusting others tend to grow gradually more suspicious. Low-trust organizations do not and cannot accomplish very much. Without trust, families, congregations, and society itself will fall apart.

Diagnosing Organizational Trust

Do individuals enmeshed in low-trust organizations know what's wrong? Shaw says yes, though the suspicion in which they are drowning often becomes a taboo subject, undiscussed and undiscussable. In fact, if you want to assess the level of trust or distrust in your organization, you might make a list of all the group's taboo subjects. The longer the list, the greater the degree of distrust. In addition, Robert B. Shaw suggests that leaders ask themselves these diagnostic questions:

1. Which of our formal structures, practices, or policies create distrust?

2. Do any of our formal organizational norms or values evoke suspicion? Which ones? How?

3. Does the distrust that hobbles us arise from a failure to achieve results? If so, is this due primarily to individuals, to key groups, or to the organization as a whole?

4. Does the distrust arise primarily from a failure to act with integrity? Does the organization have a history of acting in ways that lack integrity? Do any key players have this history?

5. Does the distrust in our congregation stem primarily from a failure to show concern? Has the organization failed to demonstrate concern for any of its members? Have the leaders? How?

These questions may bite as we ask them. They may bite harder as we face up to some of our answers. Still they point to potential solutions. No organization can solve a problem that members deny having. Servant leaders, focused as they are on healing, can't contribute to the healing processes in their organizations until they face up to the existence of distrust, its symptoms, and its probable origins.

Here again, even against the dark background of failures and fault, the power and beauty of the Gospel message can shine out in all its radiance. Here servant leaders who are Christians can enjoy heaven's invitation of grace—the invitation to confess their broken promises, their failures to act with integrity, their hypocritical words and actions. Yes, these sins may startle our followers and us at times. Yes, the discrepancies between what we say and what we do can damage the relationships we treasure with our followers. But the blood of Jesus Christ, God's Son, works forgiveness and healing in the family of God. Rebuilding broken trust is never easy. Perhaps, in the case of some sins, rebuilding trust is not possible this side of heaven.[11] In every case, though, pardon is possible. Furthermore, under God's blessing, trust can be rebuilt in many situations. We turn now to the process of healing relationships and rebuilding trust in organizations.

Process! Process! Process!

I hate the P-word—process! I would rather push a button and find instant results popping out of the toaster oven, freshly baked, into my hands. But life doesn't often work that way. By divine design, growth is a process. Most times, physical healing is a process—the broken ankle, the sprained back, and the infected eardrum all take their time in mending. Similarly, emotional healing is—most times—a process. Neither the grief over a loved one's death nor the trauma of a lost job nor the fear that torments a car-jacking victim can be erased overnight. Likewise, rebuilding damaged trust is a process.

Writing in *The Journal for Quality and Participation*, M. J. Their notes that if we attempt to short-circuit the process, we will only increase the organization's turmoil. In the example that began this chapter, Fran found that out. Her pastor's counsel to show more patience reflected his understanding of the trust-building process. Perhaps if Fran had stayed around to listen, the pastor might have explained that to her in a clearer way.

Once servant leaders recognize the need to commit themselves to trust-building over the long term, patience will come somewhat more easily. Wheatley believes that in most organizations meaningful change is at least a three- to five-year process. She admits that this may seem impossibly long for some leaders. Still, as Mintzberg warns, "The [leader] who favors the quick fix over steady progress is destroying the organization" ("Managing Quietly," online article).

Kouzes and Posner urge leaders to "go slow to go fast." They recommend moving progressively from the easiest to the most difficult issues. That way early successes can give the organization the courage everyone needs to confront the more difficult concerns.

With the idea of a trust-building process in mind, let's look at some specific ways servant leaders can productively approach a low-trust group or organization.

Trust Building—Obliquely

As we have seen in this booklet so far, trust involves doing many fundamental things right. Shaw reminds us that the most effective approaches to building trust are often those that focus on the actions that produce trust, rather than on trust itself. In fact, sometimes a focus on trust can inadvertently raise the level of distrust! Certainly organizations moving toward increasing trust do not make discussions about trust taboo. However, followers will grow even more suspicious if they suspect the leader is trying to coerce or manipulate them into trust. All things considered, it's usually best to approach trust-building by focusing on accomplishing organizational goals, rather than by working directly on the issue.

Fran, for instance, probably should not open her next school board meeting with a lecture or pep talk about trust. Rather, she might work through the diagnostic questions on page 100. She might come up with two or three actions, based on those questions, that she personally could undertake to lower the fever pitch of the group's suspicion. She might decide to abandon the evening's formal agenda in favor of simply listening to her constituents' concerns about the group's process and/or issues related to the parish school. She could listen and paraphrase, knowing ahead of time that the conversation might be confrontational. She might even listen for any offense she has caused and apologize to the group for it. Seeing trust-building and healing as an ongoing process, Fran may want to make listening and apologizing her only agenda for this month's meeting. Robert K. Greenleaf suggests:

> The best prescription, it seems to me, is to **listen intently**, with the genuine wish to learn without judging every motive, every attitude, every reason. And one must regard what one hears—which may not be pretty in some cases—as manifestations of illness to be healed rather than error to be corrected. It is amazing what problems will melt away when all one does is listen intently, with the attitude of healer. It is possible for a parent to take the heat out of a child's temper tantrum in a matter of seconds by listening. ("Types of Leaders," p. 93, emphasis in the original)

Trust Building—Communicate Continually

People know when things aren't going well. When the head elder feuds with the pastor or when the music director has irked the tenor section of the choir, the whole congregation soon senses it. A lack of communication will only allow gasoline to continue to stream down on the fires of dissent. In the absence of full disclosure from a credible source, the grapevine will continue to churn out information. Most of the information that streams from the grapevine in times like this will be negative and just plain wrong.

One of the most remarkable things I've ever seen in a worship service relates to this. At the time, I was teaching in a parish school. A spat between the head pastor and the director of Christian education (DCE) erupted. All week long the faculty heard rumors about the argument. All anyone seemed to know for sure was that the two had exchanged angry words.

The next Sunday, after the Gospel reading, the pastor remained at the lectern. He began to apologize to the DCE and to the entire congregation, expressing remorse for the things he had said to hurt his colleague and to cause other members anxiety. The rift was eventually settled, and the pastor grew about 18 inches taller in my eyes that morning because of the courage and the concern for peace he had modeled.

Of course, an action like this could be carried out with the intention of manipulating people, of making one's self look good at the expense of the other party in the dispute. But a leader who genuinely recognizes personal wrongdoing and who expresses the authentic repentance the Holy Spirit works in the hearts of His people goes a long way toward restoring trust in the congregation.

Servant leaders also communicate openly when it comes to matters like budgets, attendance, exceptions to policies, and any other potentially emotional, nonconfidential matter of parish business. Sometimes leaders withhold information, fearful that constituents will panic or abandon the organization at the first sight of bad news. The truth is that people face bad news in their everyday lives all the time and usually deal with it responsibly. When leaders hide the truth from followers in a misguided effort to "protect" them, followers usually sense the tension and guess at its root cause. Often the fears created by their guessing are worse than the truth. Deceit communicates disrespect and mistrust to followers.

Bottom line: To build trust, tell the truth—the whole truth. Even if the news you share is bad, followers will find it easier to face the truth than trying to cope with the unknown.

Trust Building—Bite the Bullet

Sometimes rebuilding trust calls for decisive action. For instance, if the sixth grade teacher is having an affair with the principal in the parish school, both need to be put on administrative leave until the pastor and elders can deal with them in the way Matthew 18 dictates. This is not vindictive. Each leader involved must balance these twin goals:

- concern for the offending faculty members and their families;

- concern for the congregation, especially for the parents and students who trust and rely on the spiritual leaders in the school.

I have seen congregations ignore situations like this, pretending only a handful of people know about the scandal. I have seen leaders hope that the necessity to take action will simply go away. It almost never does. The longer congregational leaders wait to take action, the more follower distrust will grow. However, when leaders follow the process of healing and restoration Jesus gave us in Matthew 18, their followers will have more confidence in them.

Accountability creates and sustains trust in less serious circumstances as well. Perhaps current procedures are eroding trust. Leaders should acknowledge this and replace those procedures. If individuals in the congregation have fallen into habits of gossip or if they continually backbite and criticize, leaders need to confront this behavior face-to-face and in love. In any case, Robert B. Shaw recommends that leaders act boldly to disrupt "business as usual" whenever the usual ways of doing business have broken down or become warped. He also cautions against taking a piecemeal approach to problems. Once a leader has listened thoroughly, analyzed carefully, and prayed confidently for wisdom and grace, he or she needs to take integrated action to address integrated sets of personal, structural, or cultural problems in the organization.

Trust Building—Persuasion vs. Coercion

The bold actions suggested above need to take place in the frame of persuasion. Remember, servant leaders value the freedom and dignity of their followers to such an extent that they refuse to coerce or manipulate them. This is what servant leadership is all about—building voluntary and durable consensus. Servant leaders act as catalysts to bring about this kind of consensus, a consensus built on trust.

Bernard Bass, the founding editor of *Leadership Quarterly*, calls this process "power sharing." Leaders who share power involve followers in the processes of planning and decision-making. Kouzes and Posner contend that power sharing will eventually eliminate the power struggles that plague low-trust organizations. They suggest that leaders work toward "accumulating yeses." It changes relationships when people say yes to one another. Therefore, servant leaders look for opportunities to say yes as often as possible. In addition, Kouzes and Posner suggest that leaders replace the words "Yes, but . . . " with the words "Yes, and . . . " Again, note that the technique alone, apart from a heartfelt commitment to consensus and community building, becomes only a gimmick. Resorting to techniques—even the best techniques—only to manipulate followers will destroy the trust you want to build.

Trust Building—Dealing with Resistance

After working with the voters' assembly for two years, Pastor Harris had started to feel hopeful. Members had begun to address issues openly, while the gossip and the coalition building that had created a culture of distrust before Pastor Harris's tenure had all but disappeared.

Then, the first Monday evening in October, as Pastor Harris walked into the fellowship hall, he felt his heart begin to pound. About twice the usual number of voters had shown up. Everyone was standing around in tight little clutches, four or five people each. The group seemed divided into the same coalitions that Pastor Harris thought had been eliminated months ago. He sighed and muttered under his breath, "Here we go again."

Scenes like these can discourage servant leaders, sometimes to the point of giving up. Just when you think you have made progress toward developing a Great Group, the progress seems to fall apart. Trust deteriorates. You find yourself standing at square one, or at least that's how it feels.

At times like that, I find it helpful to know what the experts tell us—remission and resistance are part of the learning process. Family therapists have long noted the powerful pull the familiar can exert on clients who are determined to change, to heal. Groups aren't much different. In times of stress or fear especially, even an emerging Great Group can fall back into familiar patterns of thinking and acting, even when they recognize how destructive those patterns can be. What can leaders do during times of resistance or remission? Greenleaf advises:

> If you see the impediment to group effectiveness as **illness**, you have a chance to enter the relationship as **healer**, as one who seeks to make whole— to make everybody whole, including yourself, the healer—so that **all** may see more clearly where they should go and how to get there.
>
> I am not arguing the general proposition that there is no error that needs to be changed or corrected. My only point is that it is a sounder attitude to enter the person/team relationship as a healer rather than a change agent. Not only is it a more effective approach, but one is less likely to fall into the trap of playing God. ("Types of Leaders," pp. 92-93, emphases in the original)

A physician, upon finding that a recovering patient has spiked a fever anew, does not panic or become angry. At least, such a response will do no good—and it might very well do harm if it evokes a reciprocal response of panic or anger in the patient. In a similar way, a servant leader holds the possibility of remission or regression in the back of her mind, knowing that if or when it happens, a healer need not panic. Instead, we need to remind ourselves that trust depends on understanding and that everyone needs to work together if the organization is to sustain gains.

Remember the advice Fran's pastor gave her about her relationship with the parish school board earlier in this chapter? Patience! Servant leaders intent on healing need not meet followers' questions or setbacks in anger or fear. As soon as you stoop to the level of the frightened, you lose your ability to lead toward success.

Instead, you can adopt a demeanor that instills confidence:

- Breathe slowly and evenly. Long, deep breaths will give everyone a chance to pause before reacting. Be sure to use body language to send the right signals. Everyone will be reading you as leader, and up to 65 percent of the message you send flows from your posture, your position in the room, and your facial expressions. When one's words don't match one's nonverbal behavior, people tend to believe the nonverbal signals rather than the words.

- Speak clearly, deliberately, and in soothing tones. Don't be condescending, but do maintain eye contact with group members individually.

Kouzes and Posner add several more helpful techniques:

- As you respond to what others say, use descriptive

rather than evaluative comments. (E.g., A comment such as "Jim, you're concerned about whether or not we'll be able to pay our bills" will signal that you have heard Jim's concerns. In contrast, a comment such as "You know, Jim, worry over money is sinful" will likely make Jim angrier. You may need to deal with sin, but in many cases you will want to do it one-on-one. After the fire of anger has been extinguished, Jim will more readily admit his need for forgiveness.)

- Ask questions for clarification. Work toward a genuine understanding of what each group member is saying and feeling. This will help you communicate your concern as healer rather than stir up defensiveness in the hearts of your followers.

- Avoid game playing in favor of spontaneity and authenticity. (E.g., Don't offer flippant or gratuitous compliments. Instead, express genuine appreciation and thankfulness when the opportunity arises.)

Finally, remember that effective, long-lasting healing and learning are accomplished interactively as people work together. Leaders who value healing allow for the process of growth rather than taking over for followers in difficult times. Letting the process work builds trust in the long run, despite the pain it may deliver in the present:

> Listening is a healing attitude of intensely holding the belief . . . that the person or persons being listened to will rise to the challenge of grappling with the issues involved in finding their own wholeness. (Greenleaf, "Religious Leaders as Seekers and Servants," p. 95)

Guided by God's grace and upheld by it, we can serve His people as His agents of healing, even when groups fall back into mistrust on occasion.[12]

Where We've Been and Where We're Headed

Trust is a powerful but fragile organizational asset. Servant leaders recognize its importance and zealously nurture the process by which it develops. They communicate openly and continuously, act with decisive boldness when trust is threatened, use persuasion rather than coercion or manipulation, and deal wisely with resistance. Most important, servant leaders see themselves as healers, not as change agents, in their organizations. This perspective helps the servant leader act in compassion and avoid discouragement. It provides peace and joy on the journey toward wholeness and healing among Christ's people.

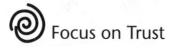 Focus on Trust

1. In what ways do you see trust as an organizational asset? What attitudes and actions related to trust does framing it in the context of organizational assets suggest?

2. Think about the fact that the Lord nowhere commands us to trust anyone but Himself.

   • Does that mean we should never trust our followers? Other leaders? Explain.

   • What does the absence of such a command in Scripture say to servant leaders in light of our need for followers' trust?

3. Work through the diagnostic questions on page 100 with your group, committee, or congregation in mind.

   • What insights do you gain?

   • If trust lies along a continuum from total trust to complete distrust, where does your group's trust level fall? Why do you think so? What clues does that give you for your role as healer?

4. Why is the healing process apt to feel discouraging at times? What hope can you take from recognizing that, most of the time, healing is a process, not an instantaneous occurrence?

5. Which of the trust-building techniques that end the chapter make the most sense to you? Which seem less sensible or practical in your present situation? Why? What might you do instead?

6. What will you carry away from this chapter into your relationships in your organization today? How—specifically—will you put your insights into practice?

Notes

1 Milton Rokeach first distinguished between "instrumental values" and "terminal values." Instrumental values deal with preferable conduct, while terminal values focus on desired end states of existence. I have chosen to state the servant-leader values in this booklet series as terminal values, because I believe that most of the various servant-leader values listed in the servant-leader literature I have studied can be considered instrumental values. I believe it is possible to subsume most, if not all of these many instrumental values under a handful of terminal values—the ones listed on these pages. For a fuller discussion of this issue, see my *Servant Leadership: Setting Leaders Free* (CPH, 2001).

2 I have rearranged their facts, changed names and places, and taken other steps to disguise the identities of the people involved to protect their anonymity and privacy.

3 Do followers owe their leaders in the church respect and honor? Undoubtedly. Scripture repeats this duty again and again (e.g., 1 Thessalonians 5:12–13; 1 Timothy 5:17–20; Hebrews 13:13, 17). People in our culture have seemingly all but lost the concept of respect for an *office* or position due respect. Instead, we tend to focus on the *office holder* when deciding whether or not to show someone honor. Perhaps the simplest way to explain the biblical concept of office is by using a military analogy. Soldiers and sailors salute the uniform, not the person wearing it. They show the *office* respect, not necessarily *the officer.* Even so, would you willingly follow an empty uniform into battle, someone who demands a show of

respect at every turn? Or would you rather follow a servant leader whose character and competence have earned your trust?

4 From an unpublished study done by the Protestant-owned Church Publishers Association for the constituent publishing houses.

5 The first booklet in this series, *Servant Leadership: Setting Leaders Free,* deals with the process of developing a vision, whether for a small team or a large and complex organization. You will want to read it if you've never guided a group through the vision-building process before or if you want to review some steps and approaches servant leaders often find helpful.

6 You may want to read *Encouraging the Heart* by Kouzes and Posner for specific and creative ways to celebrate group successes.

7 Scholars are still discussing the relationship between transformational leadership and servant leadership. That argument lies beyond the scope of this booklet. I see many parallels between the two, with servant leadership being more deeply and consciously anchored in specific and transcendent moral values. See Burns, *Leadership*, for a thorough introduction to transformational leadership. Bernard Bass has helped to popularize Burns's theories over the past few decades. In particular, you may want to read *Leadership and Performance Beyond Expectations* (London: Collier Macmillan, 1985).

8 For example, see Luke 10:7; 1 Corinthians 9:14; Galatians 6:6–7; 1 Timothy 5:17–18; 1 Thessalonians 5:12–13; and Hebrews 13:17.

9 Large size does not, in and of itself, ensure effectiveness. In *Natural Church Development: A Guide to Eight Essential Qualities of Healthy Churches,* Christian Schwarz cites evidence that, on a per-member basis, smaller congregations evangelize far more unbelievers and integrate them into

membership in the local church than do very large churches. If you serve a small- or intermediate-sized church, take heart!

10 If a group needs to implement the solution to a specific, simple problem, it is often best to let the group make the decision. While decision making will take longer, the group will be more willing to work at the implementation process.

11 For instance, given growing scientific evidence that pedophilia is probably incurable, congregations should not, in my opinion, allow child molesters to serve in any capacity in which they could possibly come into contact with children or youth.

12 In "On the Path to Servant Leadership," Lawrence Lad and David Luechauer point out that not every individual wants to grow, to become able to trust the group, or to be empowered. Judith Sturnick adds in "Healing Leadership" that not all unhealthy organizations want to heal. She goes on to point out the dangers sick groups pose for leaders who are themselves healing or already fairly healthy, suggesting a process such leaders might use in deciding whether or not to leave such an organization. That discussion lies beyond the scope of this series. Leaders facing that kind of difficult choice may find Sturnick's comments helpful.

Reference List

Adams, Bill, and Cindy Adams. "Leaders as Stewards." *Executive Excellence* 17, no. 1:8.

Atwater, David and Bernard Bass. "Transformational Leadership in Teams." In *Improving Organizational Effectiveness through Transformational Leadership*, edited by Bernard Bass and Bruce Avolio, 48–82. Thousand Oaks, Calif.: Sage Publications, 1994.

Bass, Bernard. "Transformation Leadership and Team and Organizational Decision Making." In *Improving Organizational Effectiveness through Transformational Leadership*, edited by Bernard Bass and Bruce Avolio, 104–20. Thousand Oaks, Calif.: Sage Publications, 1990.

Bennis, Warren. "Becoming a Leader of Leaders." In *Rethinking the Future*, edited by Rowan Gibson, 148–62. London: Nicholas Brealey, 1998.

_____. *Managing People Is Like Herding Cats*. Provo, Utah: Executive Excellence Publishing, 1997.

_____. *On Becoming a Leader*. Reading, Mass.: Addison-Wesley, 1989.

_____. "The Secrets of Great Groups." *Leader to Leader* 3 (Winter 1997).
http://drucker.org/leaderbooks/121/winter97/bennis.html

Blake, Robert, and Jane Mouton. *The Managerial Grid*. Houston: Gulf Publishing, 1968.

Brockner, Joel, Phyllis A. Siegel, Joseph P. Daly, Tom Tyler, and Christopher Martin. "When Trust Matters: The Moderating Effect of Outcome Favorability." *Administrative Science Quarterly* 42, no. 3: 558–83.

Burns, James McGregor. *Leadership*. New York: Harper and Row, 1978.

Cadwell, Charles. *Team Up for Success: Building Teams in the Workplace*. Des Moines: American Media Publishing, 1997.

Deep, Sam, and Lyle Sussman. *Smart Moves for People in Charge: 130 Checklists to Help You Be a Better Leader*. Reading, Mass.: Addison-Wesley, 1995.

DePree, Max. "The Leader's Legacy." *Leader to Leader* 6 (Fall 1997).

http://drucker.org/leaderbooks/121/fall97/depree.html

Deutsch, Morton. *The Resolution of Conflict: Constructive and Destructive Processes*. New Haven, Conn.: Yale University Press, 1973.

Ellis, Donald, and Aubrey Fisher. *Small-group Decision-making: Communication and the Group Process*. 4th ed. New York: McGraw-Hill, 1994.

Fassel, Diane. "Lives in the Balance: The Challenge of Servant Leaders in a Workaholic Society." In *Insights on Leadership: Service, Stewardship, Spirit, and Servant-Leadership*, edited by Larry Spears, 216–28. New York: John Wiley and Sons, 1998.

Finkelstein, Sydney, and Donald Hambrick. *Strategic Leadership: Top Executives and Their Effects on Organizations*. Minneapolis: West Publishing, 1996.

Fisher, Kimball. *Leading Self-directed Work Teams: A Guide to Developing New Team Leadership Skills*. New York: McGraw-Hill, 1993.

Fitz-enz, Jac. *The Eight Practices of Exceptional Companies: How Great Organizations Make the Most of Their Human Assets*. New York: American Management Association, 1997.

Frick, Don. "Understanding Robert K. Greenleaf and Servant Leadership." In *Insights on Leadership: Service, Stewardship, Spirit, and Servant-Leadership*, edited by Larry Spears,

353–60. New York: John Wiley and Sons, 1998.

Fryar, Jane. *Servant Leadership: Setting Leaders Free.* St. Louis: Concordia Publishing House, 2001.

Goldhaber, Gerald M. *Organizational Communication.* 6th ed. Boston: McGraw-Hill, 1993.

Greenleaf, Robert K. "Religious Leaders as Seekers and Servants. In *Seeker and Servant,* edited by Anne Fraker and Larry Spears, 9–48. San Francisco: Jossey-Bass, 1996.

————. *Servant Leadership: A Journey into the Nature of Legitimate Power and Greatness.* New York: Paulist Press, 1977.

————. "Servant: Retrospect and Prospect." In *The Power of Servant Leadership*, edited by Larry Spears, 77–92. San Francisco: Berrett-Koehler, 1998.

————. "The Leadership Crisis." In *The Power of Servant Leadership*, edited by Larry Spears, 17–60. San Francisco: Berrett-Koehler, 1998.

————."The Servant as Religious Leader." In T*he Power of Servant Leadership,* edited by Larry Spears, 111–67. San Francisco: Berrett-Koehler, 1998.

————. "Types of Leaders." In *Seeker and Servant,* edited by Anne Fraker and Larry Spears, 89–100. San Francisco: Jossey-Bass, 1973.

Handy, Charles. "The Search for Meaning." *Leader to Leader* 5 (Summer 1997).
http://drucker.org/leaderbooks/121/summer97/handy.html

Janis, Irving. *Groupthink: Psychological Studies of Policy Decisions and Fiascoes.* Boston: Houghton Mifflin, 1986.

Kaplan, Robert, and David Norton. *The Balanced Scorecard: Translating Strategy into Action.* Boston: Harvard Business School, 1996.

Kouzes, James. "Trust: The Invaluable Asset." *In Insights on Leadership: Service, Stewardship, Spirit, and Servant-*

Leadership, edited by Larry Spears, 322–4. New York: John Wiley and Sons, 1998.

Kouzes, James, and Barry Posner. *Credibility: How Leaders Gain and Lose It, Why People Demand It.* San Francisco: Jossey-Bass, 1993.

_____. *Encouraging the Heart.* San Francisco: Jossey-Bass, 1999.

_____. *The Leadership Challenge.* San Francisco: Jossey-Bass, 1995.

Lad, Lawrence, and David Luechauer. "On the Path to Servant Leadership." In *Insights on Leadership: Service, Stewardship, Spirit, and Servant-Leadership,* edited by Larry Spears, 54–67. New York: John Wiley and Sons, 1998.

Lowe, Jack. "Trust: The Invaluable Asset." In *Insights on Leadership: Service, Stewardship, Spirit, and Servant-Leadership,* edited by Larry Spears, 68–76. New York: John Wiley and Sons, 1998.

March, James, and Herbert Simon. *Organizations.* New York: John Wiley and Sons, 1958.

McCollum, Jeffrey. "The Inside-out Proposition: Finding (and Keeping) Our Balance in Contemporary Organizations." In *Insights on Leadership: Service, Stewardship, Spirit, and Servant-Leadership,* edited by Larry Spears, 326–39. New York: John Wiley and Sons, 1998.

McDonough, E. F. "Investigation of Factors Contributing to the Success of Cross-functional Teams." *Journal of Product Innovation Management* 17, no. 3: 221–35.

McGee-Cooper, Ann. "Accountability as Covenant: The Taproot of Servant Leadership." In *Insights on Leadership: Service, Stewardship, Spirit, and Servant-Leadership,* edited by Larry Spears, 77–85. New York: John Wiley and Sons, 1998.

Melrose, Ken. "Leader as Servant." *Executive Excellence* 13, no. 4: 20.

_____. "Putting Servant Leadership into Practice." In *Insights on Leadership: Service, Stewardship, Spirit, and Servant-Leadership*, edited by Larry Spears, 279–96. New York: John Wiley and Sons, 1998.

Mintzberg, Henry. "Managing Quietly." *Leader to Leader* 12 (Spring 1999). http://drucker.org/leaderbooks/l2l/spring99/mintzberg.html

Orlikoff, James, and Mary Totten. "Building and Maintaining Trust: The Role of Leadership." *Trustee* 52, no. 7: T1-T4.

Pfeffer, Jeffrey. "The Real Keys to High Performance." *Leader to Leader* 8 (Spring 1998). http://drucker.org/leaderbooks/l2l/spring98/pfeffer.html

Putnam, Robert D. *Bowling Alone: The Collapse and Revival of American Communities.* New York: Simon and Schuster, 2000.

Rokeach, Milton. *Beliefs, Attitudes, and Values: A Theory of Organization and Change.* San Francisco: Jossey-Bass, 1969.

Russell, Robert. "Exploring the Values and Attributes of Servant Leaders." Unpublished manuscript, Regent University—Center for Leadership Studies, 1999.

Shaw, Robert B. *Trust in the Balance: Building Successful Organizations on Results, Integrity, and Concern.* San Francisco: Jossey-Bass, 1997.

Schein, Edgar. *Organizational Culture and Leadership.* 2d ed. San Francisco: Jossey-Bass, 1992.

Schrage, Michael. *No More Teams! Mastering the Dynamics of Creative Collaboration.* New York: Doubleday, 1995.

Schwarz, Christian. *Natural Church Development: A Guide to Eight Essential Qualities of Healthy Churches.* Carol Stream, Ill.: Church Smart Resources, 1998.

Senge, Peter. "Through the Eye of the Needle." In *Rethinking the Future*, edited by Ron Gibson, 122–46. London: Nicholas Brealey, 1998.

Spears, Larry. "Tracing the Growing Impact of Servant Leadership." In *The Power of Servant Leadership*, edited by Larry Spears, 1–12. San Francisco: Berrett-Koehler, 1998.

Stone, Gregory, and Bruce Winston. "Theory S: A Values-based Theory of Management and Leadership Focusing on People and Results." Unpublished manuscript, Regent University—Center for Leadership Studies, 1998.

Sturnick, Judith. "Healing Leadership." In *Insights on Leadership: Service, Stewardship, Spirit, and Servant-Leadership*, edited by Larry Spears, 185–93. New York: John Wiley and Sons, 1998.

Temkin, Terrie. "Nonprofit Leadership: New Skills Are Needed." *Nonprofit World* 12, no. 5: 35–45.

Their, M. J. "Create Success Out of Chaos." *The Journal for Quality and Participation* 18, no. 5: 6–10.

Wheatley, Margaret. "Goodbye, Command and Control." *Leader to Leader* 5 (Summer 1997). http://drucker.org/leaderbooks/121/summer97/wheatley.html

Wicks, Andrew, Shawn Berman, and Thomas Jones. "The Structure of Optimal Trust: Moral and Strategic Implications." *Academy of Management Review* 24, no. 1: 99–116.

Yukl, Gary. *Leadership in Organizations*. 4th ed. Upper Saddle River, N.J.: Prentice-Hall, 1998.

Servant Leadership

by Jane L. Fryar
80 pages 5" x 7-1/2"
perfect-bound
0-570-06770-7   12-4121GNP
$7.99 ($12.50 Can.)   (B)

Many today misconstrue the idea of leadership. Some in the church load it with connotations of supremacy, privilege, and power. Perhaps we covet positions of leadership so that we can have our own way or so that others will honor us. Perhaps our love of power reveals our sinful nature, ever rebelling against our Lord. But today Jesus still lives among us as "the One who serves." He not only modeled a better way of life and of true leadership for us; He sacrificed Himself on the cross and rose again to remove the guilt of our selfishness and sinful pride.

Servant Leadership explores a better model than current "trait-based" and "behavior-based" theories of leadership. This "values-based" theory of leadership can trace its roots to the descriptions of godly leadership in the Old Testament.

Available through your local Christian bookstore.

CPH
Concordia Publishing House
www.cph.org